Steroids
Pumped Up and Dangerous

ILLICIT AND MISUSED DRUGS

ILLICIT AND MISUSED DRUGS

Steroids
Pumped Up
and Dangerous

by Ida Walker

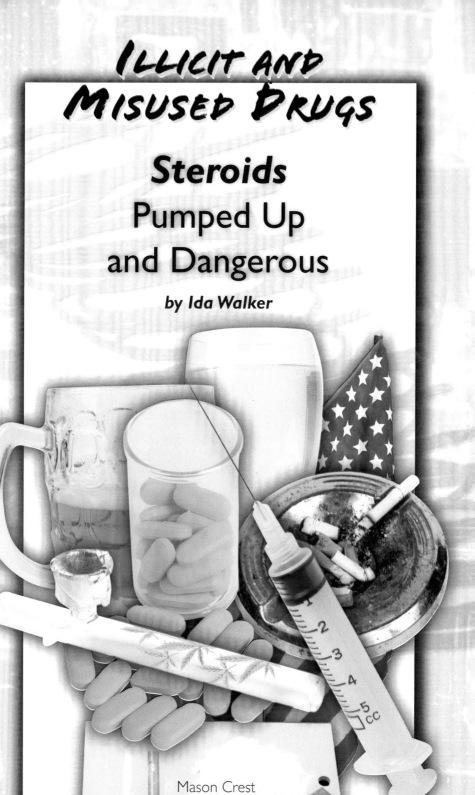

Mason Crest

Mason Crest
370 Reed Road
Broomall, Pennsylvania 19008
www.masoncrest.com

Printed in the Hashemite Kingdom of Jordan.

First printing
9 8 7 6 5 4 3 2 1

Library of Congress Cataloging-in-Publication Data

Walker, Ida.
Steroids : pumped up and dangerous / by Ida Walker.
    p. cm. — (Illicit and misused drugs)
Includes bibliographical references and index.
ISBN 978-1-4222-2441-0 (hardcover : alk. paper)
ISBN 978-1-4222-2424-3 (hardcover series : alk. paper)
ISBN 978-1-4222-9305-8 (ebook)
1. Steroids—Physiological effect. 2. Steroid abuse. 3. Doping in sports. I. Title.
 HV5822.S68W35 2012
 362.29'9—dc23
                                        2011042730

Interior design by Benjamin Stewart.
Cover design by Torque Advertising + Design.
Produced by Harding House Publishing Services, Inc.
www.hardinghousepages.com

This book is meant to educate and should not be used as an alternative to appropriate medical care. Its creators have made every effort to ensure that the information presented is accurate—but it is not intended to substitute for the help and services of trained professionals.

CONTENTS

INTRODUCTION

Addicting drugs are among the greatest challenges to health, well-being, and the sense of independence and freedom for which we all strive—and yet these drugs are present in the everyday lives of most people. Almost every home has alcohol or tobacco waiting to be used, and has medicine cabinets stocked with possibly outdated but still potentially deadly drugs. Almost everyone has a friend or loved one with an addiction-related problem. Almost everyone seems to have a solution neatly summarized by word or phrase: medicalization, legalization, criminalization, war-on-drugs.

For better and for worse, drug information seems to be everywhere, but what information sources can you trust? How do you separate misinformation (whether deliberate or born of ignorance and prejudice) from the facts? Are prescription drugs safer than "street" drugs? Is occasional drug use really harmful? Is cigarette smoking more addictive than heroin? Is marijuana safer than alcohol? Are the harms caused by drug use limited to the users? Can some people become addicted following just a few exposures? Is treatment or counseling just for those with serious addiction problems?

These are just a few of the many questions addressed in this series. It is an empowering series because it provides the information and perspectives that can help people come to their own opinions and find answers to the challenges posed by drugs in their own lives. The series also provides further resources for information and assistance, recognizing that no single source has all the answers. It should be of interest and relevance to areas of study spanning biology, chemistry, history, health, social studies and more. Its efforts to provide a real-world context for the information that is clearly presented but not overly simplified should be appreciated by students, teachers, and parents.

The series is especially commendable in that it does not pretend to pose easy answers or imply that all decisions can be made on the basis of simple facts: some challenges have no immediate or simple solutions, and some solutions will need to rely as much upon basic values as basic facts. Despite this, the series should help to at least provide a foundation of knowledge. In the end, it may help as much by pointing out where the solutions are not simple, obvious, or known to work. In fact, at many points, the reader is challenged to think for him- or herself by being asked what his or her opinion is.

A core concept of the series is to recognize that we will never have all the facts, and many of the decisions will never be easy. Hopefully, however, armed with information, perspective, and resources, readers will be better prepared for taking on the challenges posed by addictive drugs in everyday life.

— *Jack E. Henningfield, Ph.D.*

1 Steroids: An Easy Answer?

Every time he passed a mirror, Craig flexed his muscles. He wanted to look "insanely big—like an action figure."

It all started when Craig was 18. Before a trip to Walt Disney World in Orlando, Florida, he was feeling overweight. He wanted to look good with his shirt off, so he resolved to get fit. . . . Running on the treadmill, he slimmed down fast, losing 20 pounds in a month.

But lean wasn't Craig's ideal. "My whole priority was, I wanted people to say, *That guy's huge.*"

He lifted weights and experimented with steroidal supplements. . . . These drugs promise to build muscles. Despite potential risks and unclear effectiveness, they can be bought legally over the counter at many stores.

But what Craig was looking for couldn't be bought in a store. So he turned to anabolic steroids. . . .

Women are not the only ones who feel pressured to conform to cultural images of physical beauty; males may also experience feelings of insecurity because of their physical appearance. Some young men turn to steroids as a way to change their body structure.

Craig, whose story is told on the website teens. drugabuse.gov/stories, is not unlike many individuals': he wasn't happy with the way he looked. At first glance, one might assume that if we're hearing about someone who is unhappy with appearance, it has to be a girl. Most guys care about how they look, too. And some, like Craig, choose an unhealthy way to improve their appearance—anabolic steroids.

What Are Steroids?

Steroids are naturally occurring hormones in the body. Although all steroids are **lipids** composed of a carbon skeleton with four fused rings attached, steroids differ in what functions are attached to the rings. Researchers have identified hundreds of steroids in plant, animal, and fungal life.

In the human body, steroids act as hormones. When steroids attach to steroid receptor proteins, cells adapt to fight stress, promote growth, and bring on puberty, the stage of development at which individuals become capable of sexual reproduction.

Those are the naturally occurring steroids, not the type Craig and many others use to enhance their appearance. Instead, the steroids these individuals are interested in are the **synthetic** ones called anabolic-androgenic steroids: anabolic referring to their muscle-building properties and androgenic referring to their ability to increase masculine characteristics (androgens are the male-type sex hormones in the body). In the case of anabolic-androgenic steroids, often just called anabolic steroids, the word "steroids" indicates the class of drugs. Unless otherwise noted, these are the steroids discussed in this book.

Miracle Cures or Snake-Oil Salesmen

Steroid manufacturers who make false claims come from a long ancestry of unfulfilled medical promises. In the late 1800s, medicine show "professors" traveled around North America, hawking their miraculous, exotic "cures" from soapboxes or platforms in carnival tents. These medicine men brought North America everything from Foley's Honey and Tar (for coughs and colds) to Hot Springs Liver Buttons (which promised to keep "your liver all right and your bowels regular"). The audience listened and purchased these cures because the products promised "health in a bottle" during a time of limited access to good medical care.

According to Dr. Tina Brewster Wray, the Curator of Collections at the White River Valley Museum in Auburn, Washington, medicine merchants marketed over 100,000 brands of patent medicines between 1860 and 1900. But these so-called cures were nothing new.

Patent medicines arrived in North America in the late 1700s as medicines that had been produced under grants from the English king. Under these grants, which were called "patents," the king gave his official permission for the manufacturer to develop the medicine, and he promised to provide royal financial backing. Hence the name, "patent medicine." The actual medicines (their recipe and ingredient list) weren't patented in North America as we think of patents today; only the medicine's name and packaging were registered with the government as a trademark to protect the remedy's owner and manufacturer. The ingredient list and recipe remained secret. And that was a problem.

Most patent medicine ingredients weren't medicines at all. Though they claimed to cure everything from diaper rash to diabetes, they were often nothing more than alcohol, flavorings, herbs, or narcotics mixed together and put into a colorful bottle or box with an impressive-looking label. Some of the more popular patent medicines included:

- Lydia Pinkham's Vegetable Compound, a brew of herbs and alcohol, claimed to treat menstrual cramps and cure other women's ills.
- Hamlin's Wizard Oil Company's cure-all, The Great Medical Wonder, promised to cure headaches within five minutes, earaches in ten, and nerve disorders in fifteen. Its advertisements read, "There is no Sore it will Not Heal, No Pain it will not subdue."
- Dr. William's Pink Pills for Pale People was advertised to be a "safe and effective tonic for the blood and nerves." Its label claimed that the pills treated anemic conditions, nervous disorders, and conditions caused by thin blood.

Anabolic steroids are synthetic **derivatives** of testosterone, the sex hormone produced by specialized cells in the testicles in the male and by the adrenal glands in both males and females (though in much smaller quantity than what is produced in the testicles). The credit for discovering testosterone is given to Charles Edouard Brown, who reported in 1889 that he had reversed the aging process by injecting himself with liquid derived from the testicles of dogs and guinea pigs.

Testosterone is the most important androgen. It promotes the development of masculine characteristics that

Testosterone causes secondary sexual characteristics in males, including the growth of facial hair.

occurs during puberty. When a boy's voice cracks and then gets deeper, and when he starts growing body hair, that's a sign that his testosterone levels have increased, and he is entering puberty. Testosterone can also affect how aggressive someone is and the level of an individual's sex drive. And just as males have small levels of the female hormones estrogen and progesterone in their makeup, female bodies have small amounts of testosterone. Some athletes, hoping to increase the possibility of

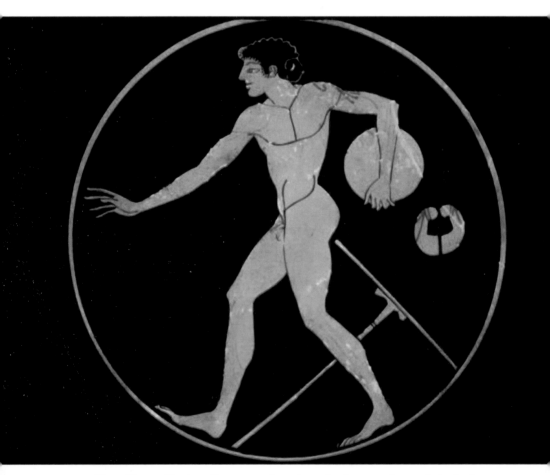

The athletes of Ancient Greece may have been the first to enhance their physical performance with testicular and plant extracts.

Hitler and Steroids

In 1935, researchers in Germany studying dogs discovered that the male hormone testosterone could increase muscle mass. Before then, the relationship of steroids and muscle mass was not known. Stories have persisted that German dictator Adolf Hitler took advantage of his countrymen's discovery by ordering that some of his troops be given steroids to increase their size, strength, and fighting ability. Although it makes for an interesting story, there is no definitive proof that it actually took place.

success, have resorted to taking these steroids to increase their strength and muscle mass.

Steroidal supplements are another group of steroids. These substances contain either dehydroepiandrosterone (DHEA) or androstenedione (also called andro); some contain both. Steroidal supplements are often sold at health-food stores and gyms. Not much is known about the effects of DHEA- and andro-containing supplements, but some in the scientific community believe that when taken in large doses, they can result in effects similar to testosterone. The long-term effect of many of these steroidal supplements is another area of mystery. The one thing that is known with certainty is that many manufacturers of such products make claims that are not true.

The History of Anabolic Steroids

Although steroids have often been in the news during the past few years, they are not a new discovery, and neither is the desire to perform and look better. Some researchers have suggested that even the athletes of Ancient Greece took a little something to give an added boost to their performance level, and to heighten their masculinity.

Researchers hypothesize that these athletes used testicular and plant extracts in their search for peak performance.

Historically, **Western** medicine has long been interested in finding ways to increase the body's performance, but in the early years it was sexual performance, not athletic ability, people wanted to enhance. In Eastern medicine, especially that practiced in China, intense research looked into ways to increase potency in males. In their striving to find the perfect supplements, Chinese medical practitioners used ingredients as varied as deer antler, tiger bone, bear gallbladder, and plants such as ginseng. Though some still claim that these substances are effective, no scientific evidence proves that they increase male sexual performance.

The relationship between sports and steroids first appeared in the United States just three years after its discovery. A letter to the editor in *Strength and Health*, a magazine targeted at weightlifters and bodybuilders, mentions the effects of testosterone propinate. This oil-based, injectable steroid is still available in Europe.

During the 1940s, researchers discovered that androgens such as testosterone had qualities that could relieve pain, increase appetite, and give one a sense of well-being. Researchers studied the **efficacy** of testosterone in the treatment of **hypogonadism**, **impotence**, and advanced cancer. According to research done on the history of

HIV/AIDS treatments, scientists even used testosterone treatments in an attempt to change sexual orientation. When treatments were conducted on male homosexuals, however, their **libido** increased, but their sexual orientation remained the same. Since the 1940s, testosterone and steroids have been used in boys to stimulate growth and puberty when development is slowed.

Americans did not take much interest in steroids for almost twenty years after their discovery. Then, in 1956, John Ziegler developed methandrostenolone, and pharmaceutical manufacturer Ciba marketed the drug under the brand name Dianabol (D-bol or d-bol). Initially,

Dianabol was used to improve weightlifters' performance.

Drug Approval

Before a drug can be marketed in the United States, the Food and Drug Administration (FDA) must officially approve it. Today's FDA is the primary consumer protection agency in the United States. Operating under the authority given it by the government, and guided by laws established throughout the twentieth century, the FDA has established a rigorous drug approval process that verifies the safety, effectiveness, and accuracy of labeling for any drug marketed in the United States.

While the United States has the FDA for the approval and regulation of drugs and medical devices, Canada has a similar organization called the Therapeutic Product Directorate (TPD). The TPD is a division of Health Canada, the Canadian government's department of health. The TPD regulates drugs, medical devices, disinfectants, and sanitizers with disinfectant claims. Some of the things that the TPD monitors are quality, effectiveness, and safety. Just as the FDA must approve new drugs in the United States, the TPD must approve new drugs in Canada before those drugs can enter the market.

Dianabol use was limited to athletes in sports such as weightlifting, bodybuilding, and some field events. Although the U.S. Food and Drug Administration (FDA) forced the original formulation of Dianabol off the market because it determined the risks of use outweighed the benefits, other formulations of methandrostenolone remain popular and are still available.

For many years after the discovery of these manmade steroids, doubts existed as to whether they really did enhance performance or appearance. In a 1972 study, participants were told they would be receiving a daily injection of a steroid. Participants reported to the researchers that their performances had indeed been enhanced by the injections. However, instead of steroids, these participants had been getting daily injections of a *placebo*. Since the improved performance noted by the placebo-receiving participants was no different than what was gained by individuals taking the real steroids, many researchers believed that the steroids had no effect. However, since the study, its results have been disputed because of flaws in how it was conducted.

Another study, funded by the National Institutes of Health (NIH), was conducted in 1996. This study tested the effects of large doses of testosterone enanthate. Study subjects were given 600 milligrams a week *intramuscularly* for ten weeks. At the end of the study, participants were found to have an increase in muscle mass along with a decrease in body fat when compared with a group who took a placebo.

The Scientific Method

Scientists must follow strict guidelines and procedures when conducting experimental studies. This is called the scientific method, the process by which scientists working independently and together, over time, construct a reliable, consistent, and nonarbitrary representation of the world.

To accomplish this goal, scientists use standardized procedures and criteria to minimize the influence of personal preferences and biases in interpreting findings and developing theories. There are four steps involved in the scientific method:

1. Observation and description of a phenomenon or group of phenomena.
2. Formulation of an hypothesis to explain the phenomena.
3. Use of the hypothesis to predict the existence of other phenomena, or to predict quantitatively the results of new observations.
4. Performance of experimental tests of the predictions by several independent experimenters and properly performed experiments.

Steroids are usually associated with athletes who want to "bulk up," but they also have other medical uses.

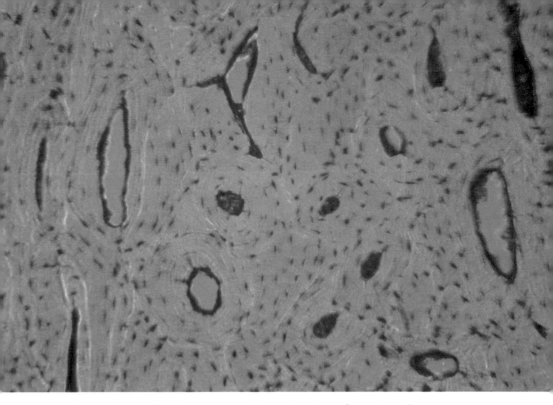

Bone marrow cells. Today a person with a serious type of anemia might receive a bone marrow transplant, but steroids were once used to stimulate the growth of bone marrow cells.

Medical Uses

Many people automatically associate steroids with "bulking up." However, these substances do have medical benefits. One of the first uses of steroids was in the treatment of chronic physical wasting in concentration camp survivors. (This is different from chronic wasting disease, a neurological disease found in deer that can be transferred to humans.) As mentioned previously, since the 1940s, steroids have been used in boys in whom puberty has been delayed. Other medical uses include:

- bone marrow stimulation: Before bone marrow transplants, steroids were often used in the treatment of **hypoplastic anemias** not caused by a nutrition deficiency.

According to some studies, a man who is taller is more apt to be successful, socially and professionally, than a man who is shorter.

A Real Medical Condition?

A September 2006 story on the CBS Evening News opened by asking viewers if Academy Award–winning actor Dustin Hoffman, renowned film director Martin Scorcese, or former labor secretary Robert Reich suffered from medical conditions. They weren't asking about cancer or hepatitis, or anything like that. The medical condition they were asking about was shortness.

It seems as though some parents do believe shortness is a medical condition that must be treated, and they are spending thousands of dollars to have their children undergo steroid therapy to gain additional inches. One boy profiled in the story had grown three inches with the treatment. Before steroid therapy, doctors had estimated he'd be 5'5" when he reached his full height. His parents thought their son would be discriminated against in employment, and might even have a difficult time finding a spouse. So, they put him on steroid therapy. His doctors now project that his full height will be 5'8".

Is shortness a medical condition that needs to be treated? Does shortness—especially in males—compromise an individual's ability to get and advance in jobs and to find a life partner? Are three additional inches worth the risks that might come with treatment?

What do you think?

- growth stimulation: Until the development of synthetic growth hormones, steroids were used to treat children whose physical growth was stunted.
- appetite stimulant: Steroids have often been prescribed for individuals with cancer and AIDS and other conditions in which the appetite may be lessened and muscle mass diminished.
- age-related problems in the elderly: Steroids have proven beneficial in the treatment of some problems associated with aging. These include diminished appetite.

Steroids are sometimes used to improve appetite in elderly patients.

Controlled Substances Act

In 1970, the U.S. Congress enacted the Controlled Substances Act (CSA) as part of the Comprehensive Drug Abuse Prevention and Control Act, an attempt to deal with the country's drug problem. The CSA is the mechanism under which the federal government regulates the manufacture, importation, possession, and distribution of certain drugs.

The CSA also led to the creation of the five drug schedules used to classify drugs. Working together, the U.S. Department of Justice and the Department of Health and Human Services decide what drugs to include on the schedules based on their potential for abuse, accepted medical uses, and the potential for addiction.

- *gender dysmorphia*: Secondary male characteristics, those that would come during puberty in males, are initiated in preparation for female-to-male reassignment.

Although no one doubted that steroids had medical uses, in 1990, the U.S. government determined that the risks involved with taking them outweighed the substances' benefits. Under the Anabolic Steroid Act of 1990, steroids were placed under the Controlled Substances Act, meaning that they were placed on the Department of Justice's Schedule of Controlled Substances. As a Schedule III drug, they are subject to specific penalties for illegal manufacture, distribution, and use.

Despite the recognized dangers of steroid abuse, many individuals continue to use these substances. These individuals make up a diverse group that includes some of the best-known athletes in the world.

2 Who Abuses Steroids— and Why and How?

It's not like I was really fat. I was a little overweight, but not a lot. It seemed like no matter how much I exercised, I just couldn't lose the fat. One day a friend told me that her brother had used steroids to make himself look more in shape. So, she got me some from her brother's stash, and I started taking them. It seemed like in no time, my body looked like I had been working out for months. Everybody noticed how great I looked—even the really popular guys. I started having a social life with lots of dates.

I figured if I keep using steroids I'd keep looking better and better. Wrong. I never really had big boobs, but what I did have seemed to shrink before my eyes. Then I started getting hairy—I mean really hairy and not just on my head. I Googled steroids and learned these were side effects of taking steroids. Well, they just weren't worth it.

Yes, females also abuse steroids. Emily's story, told in an Internet chat room, reflects an under-recognized group of steroid abusers: girls using them to lose weight and tone up. Although girls and women are in the minority of steroid users, their numbers are growing. Steroid abusers are not just the professional athletes whose names and stories are all over the media.

What Is Abuse?

As mentioned previously in this book, there are legitimate medical reasons for taking steroids. Health-care professionals write prescriptions that other professionals—pharmacists or their assistants—fill. The individual for whom the steroids have been prescribed is the person who actually takes them, and they are taken according to the instructions provided by the health-care professional.

Then there's the individual who takes steroids for reasons other than why they are prescribed. Or the person purposely takes more of them, or takes them more often than prescribed. Many times, these individuals didn't go through a health-care professional to get a prescription and have it filled. They may have gone to the gym or gotten the steroids through a friend with a prescription. Or they could have purchased steroids or supplements legitimately over the counter. The primary characteristic of abuse is that a substance is being taken in a way that was not intended by the manufacturer or health-care professional.

Not all steroid abusers are male; girls may also turn to these chemicals to help them achieve the bodies they want.

Steroids—Pumped Up and Dangerous 29

The pressure of high school sports programs encourages a small percentage of teen athletes to turn to steroids.

The Stats

Although generalizations can be made about who abuses steroids, actual statistics are sparse. Many government and other agencies that compile statistics on drug abuse in the United States do not include steroids among those drugs. This makes it difficult to obtain thorough statistics on the extent of steroid abuse in the United States.

One study that does survey the abuse of steroids is the Monitoring the Future Study (MTF). Since 1975, MTF has measured drug, alcohol, and cigarette use and related attitudes among adolescent students nationwide. Survey participants report their drug-use behaviors across three time periods: lifetime, past year, and past month. In 2011, 46,700 students in grades 8, 10, and 12 from 400 public and private schools participated in the survey. The survey is funded by the National Institute on Drug Abuse (NIDA), a component of the National Institutes of Health, and conducted by the University of Michigan.

In the 2011 MTF study, the use of any illicit drug during the previous year has steadily dropped since

Percentage of Students Reporting Steroid Use, 2011

	8th Grade	10th Grade	12th Grade
Past month	0.5	0.6	0.9
Past year	1.1	1.3	1.5
Lifetime	1.7	2.0	2.6

(*Source*: Monitoring the Future Study, 2011)

2001. The peak for drug abuse among eighth-graders was 1996, while the peak for tenth- and twelfth-graders was in 1997. Abuse of steroids has also decreased in twelfth-graders. In 2011, only 1.2 percent of those surveyed indicated they had used steroids during the past year; in 2004, 2.5 percent admitted doing so. Among eighth-graders, the reported annual use has declined—it is now 0.7 percent. There was a decrease in the number of tenth-graders reporting steroid use during the previous year.

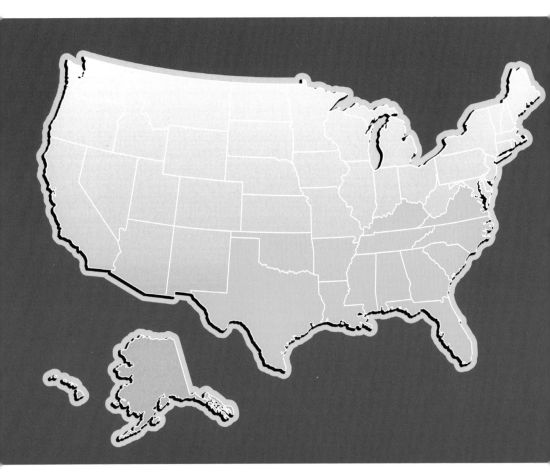

Steroid abuse is more common in the southern states.

Steroids in Canada

Although the Canadian government has acknowledged that steroid abuse is a problem there as well, like in the United States, there is little statistical information available about its prevalence. The abuse of steroids and other performance-enhancing substances has worked itself into its national sport, hockey. A 2003 report cited in an issue of the Montreal *La Presse* states that as many as 60 percent of the players in the Quebec Major Junior Hockey League had drug problems, including the abuse of steroids and performance-enhancing substances.

The 2011 study also found that more males than females reported abusing steroids; 1.8 percent of male study participants in twelfth grade reported using steroids during the previous year, while only 0.5 percent of girls reported the same.

Perhaps one of the most hopeful statistics about steroid use that came from the 2011 MTF study was in the twelfth-graders' perception of the harmfulness of steroid use. In 1998, 68.1 percent of individuals in twelfth grade reported that they believed using steroids was harmful. The percentages indicating they felt steroid use was harmful decreased to 57.9 percent in 2000. The following year, 58.9 percent reported they perceived it to be harmful. Following decreases in 2002 and 2003, however, the percentages indicating they believed steroid use was harmful increased to 61 percent by 2011.

Compared to the abuse of other drugs, the percentages of individuals using steroids is much smaller; for example, in 2011, 10.6 percent of youth surveyed reported abusing inhalants. However, because most surveys do not include steroids in their questionnaires, figures on abuse may be seriously underestimated.

Geographic location may also have a role in who abuses steroids. In a 2001 study by the Centers for Disease Control and Prevention (CDC), the South had more cases of steroid abuse than other parts of the United States.

The Individuals Behind the Stats

Originally, steroid abuse was most often found on college campuses and in Olympic and professional sports. Today, most steroid abuse continues to occur among athletes, professional and amateur. According to the American Academy of Pediatrics (www.aap.org), steroid abuse is most likely to occur within these groups:

- athletes involved in sports that rely on strength and size, like football, wrestling, or baseball
- endurance athletes, such as those involved in track-and-field and swimming
- athletes involved in weight training or bodybuilding
- anyone interested in building and defining muscles

FAST FACT

According to a 2004 article in the New York Times, some doctors estimated that between 500,000 and 1 million high school students use steroids.

The NIDA reports that between 1 percent and 6 percent of athletes may abuse steroids.

While publicity about steroid abuse has centered on college and professional athletes, they're not the only ones taking performance- and body-enhancing substances. According to the 1999

Steroids and the Olympics

A connection between steroid use and the Olympic Games can be traced back to 1964. In an attempt to increase the chances of winning a medal, athletes and trainers used high dosages of many drugs to improve the athlete's advantage (or create one where there wasn't). There was no scientific evidence to guide them; their concoction and regimen were often based on little more than anecdotal evidence, hunch, and trial and error.

As stories of these regimens circulated in the athletic community, more and more athletes began using steroids to improve their performances. As of 1991, for example, the only Olympic sports in which steroid use had not been detected were women's field hockey and figure skating.

Despite drug testing, the use of steroids among Olympic athletes has grown. The challenge for these athletes and their "handlers" has been to come up with new substances that are not covered by Olympic and sport regulations, or that can't be detected by current drug screenings. And many have succeeded.

MTF, most of the high school individuals who reported using steroids were not planning to go to college. They had their own reasons for using steroids.

Why Use Steroids?

According to the website www.coolnurse.com, teens feel pressure to use steroids because of the "nots" in their lives. For them, these are good reasons to abuse steroids:

- not making the sports team
- not meeting peer pressure and demands
- not getting "the girls"
- not being able to compete with others who are using steroids
- not looking as good as you could

Steroids and Athletes

Urine tests can reveal if an athlete has been breaking the rules by using steroids.

Steroids and athletes have gone together for centuries. Although studies may indicate that a maximum of 6 percent of athletes abuse steroids, **anecdotal evidence** suggests that the actual number is much higher.

Improving athletic performance is one of the main reasons individuals give for abusing steroids. New "designer" drugs are being developed that allow athletes—including those who compete in the Olympics and other worldwide competitions—to evade detection by current urine and blood tests. For the athlete who chooses to cheat—to have an unfair advantage—any risk of detection is outweighed by the increased possibility of grabbing a victory.

The competition to "make the team" can be intense, whether it involves a middle-school, high school, or college team. The pressures felt by these athletes can **transcend** the present. For example, the middle-school athlete may be pressured to perform well so he can get on the team in high school, get scouted and signed by a good college, and perhaps make it to the pros.

Though a professional sports career is unlikely for most athletes, that fact often goes unnoticed by the parents and coaches of young athletes, especially of those who show promise in their particular sport. According to www.coolnurse.com, these coaches and parents can pressure young athletes in the following ways:

- They often push young athletes into sports development programs.
- Glorify youngsters who are willing to risk their bodies and morals in order to win.
- Demand that young athletes aspire to greatness at any cost.

Young people grow and develop with the help of

Steroids played a tragic role in the life of footfall star Lyle Alzado, #77.

role models, and that may be especially true in sports. Even if not proven, stories of professional and high-level amateur athletes who have used performance-enhancing substances abound. Bicycle racer Lance Armstrong has been dogged by stories of alleged doping throughout most of his career. In 2006, cyclist Floyd Landis won the Tour de France, coming back from what seemed like insurmountable odds. After the awarding of the yellow jacket signifying his win, the media announced that he had tested positive for exceedingly high levels of testosterone, possibly indicating he had taken performance-enhancing drugs. He appealed the findings, but was found guilty of using steroids. In early September 2006, two members of the 1999 U.S. Tour de France team admitted using banned substances. Landis himself later publicly admitted his drug problem in 2010.

It's not just bicycle racing whose image is being tarnished by stories of steroid abuse. Many of the role mod-

A Football Giant

In 1985, Los Angeles Raider Lyle Alzado retired after an illustrious football career and a Super Bowl ring. In May 1992, he died. He was forty-three years old.

Although the official cause of death is listed as complications from lymphoma of the brain, an extremely rare form of cancer, Alzado placed part of the blame for his illness on his decades-old steroid abuse.

As a defensive end for the Denver Broncos, Cleveland Browns, and Los Angeles Raiders, Alzado weighed 254 pounds and was an intimidating force on the field. But, he hadn't always been that powerful. He played football in high school but was far from being a standout. His college career didn't start out much better—but that was when Alzado discovered steroids. And they worked. He got bigger, and he became a powerhouse for Yankton College in South Dakota.

Drafted by the Denver Broncos, Alzado began his successful career in professional football. His life was colorful, both on the field and off. He even boxed against Muhammad Ali in an exhibition match. But his steroid-induced rages were unpredictable. After his death, former teammates remarked that, while he was a terror on the field (he once ripped the helmet off opposing player Chris Ward and threatened to behead Washington Redskins' quarterback Joe Theismann), he was kind and gentle off. Some—including a selection of ex-wives and a person whose car he chased through the hills in Denver—might beg to differ with that assessment.

Throughout his playing career, Alzado had denied using steroids. But after he was diagnosed with cancer in 1991, he admitted using them since his days at Yankton College. In an interview with Sports Illustrated, Alzado admitted "I just didn't feel strong unless I was taking something." Alzado estimated that at his peak usage of steroids and human growth hormone, he was spending $30,000 a year on the drugs. Since NFL teams play half their games on the road, he bought them at gyms all over the country. And, he didn't just buy them for himself. According to Alzado, he helped keep his teammates supplied with steroids—all they had to do was ask.

There is no absolute cause-and-effect linkage between lymphoma and steroid use, but Alzado truly believed one existed. He also blamed steroid use for the career-threatening injury to his Achilles' tendon in 1983. Regardless of whether Alzado's steroid use directly led to his death, it undeniably affected his life.

els of Little Leaguers and other baseball players have found their names linked with steroid abuse. The names José Conseco, Bobby Bonds, Ken Caminiti have almost become synonymous with steroid abuse—proven or alleged. And when home-run king Mark McGwire admitted to using the supplement androstenedione, interest in it and other steroids and supplements increased. Some major leaguers even found themselves facing a congressional hearing instead of a fastball. Young athletes see the success that these and other pros have achieved, and for many, steroid and other performance-enhancing substances seem to be a necessary part of that success.

Other Reasons for Taking Steroids

Athletes are not the only ones taking steroids. Others take steroids to increase their muscle mass and decrease their amount of body fat just for appearance reasons. Although this might include athletes, including weightlifters and bodybuilders, it just as easily includes individuals who simply want to look better—the guy who wants more muscles so he'll be more attractive to the girls, a girl who wants a more toned look.

Individuals who abuse steroids for this reason also include people who have the behavioral disorder called muscle dysmorphia. People with muscle dysmorphia have a distorted body image. How the person with muscle dysmorphia sees the body depends on whether the individual is male or female. Males with the disorder see themselves as weak and small—the weakling on the beach who gets sand kicked in his face. Females with muscle dysmorphia view themselves as fat and flabby, with little or no muscle tone. In both cases, reality is the opposite of what is perceived; males can actually be strong and very muscular,

Young baseball players look to the big leagues for role models. When so many big-name stars use steroids, it's no wonder that young people turn to these chemicals as well.

A NIDA study found a connection between weightlifting, steroid abuse, and a history of sexual trauma.

and women are often lean and healthy.

Others who use steroids to increase their muscle mass have experienced some kind of abuse, usually physical or sexual, often when very young. According to a study reported by NIDA in 2005, 25 percent of male weightlifters who abused steroids had memories of abuse as a child. Female weightlifters who used steroids or other body-enhancing substances were twice as likely to have been raped than their non-steroid-using peers. Most of the female weightlifters who had been raped indicated that they had increased their bodybuilding activities, which sometimes included steroid use, after the attack. Many believed that the increased muscle mass would allow them to fight off any future attacks, or even better, prevent future attacks, since men might be intimidated or turned off by a muscular woman.

For some individuals, taking steroids and other such substances is just part of a behavior pattern. These people are well aware of the risks of taking steroids, and for them, that is a significant part of the attraction. These individuals participate in other high-risk behaviors as well. They may drive too fast, ride a motorcycle or bicycle without a helmet, carry a weapon, or abuse other substances. The risk associated with all of these activities gives them the "rush" some people seem to need to survive emotionally.

Women and Steroids

Most of the studies involving steroid abuse have dealt with males. After all, they are the ones who usually abuse these substances. Though males are still the highest abusers of steroids and other body- and performance-enhancing substances, increasing numbers of females are using them as well.

Most females who abuse steroids do so in order to achieve their image of the "perfect" body.

The number of girls and women using steroids is uncertain, with a CDC study indicating that up to 7 percent of fifteen-year-old girls had used steroids at least once, and another study reporting that the number was closer to 1 to 2 percent abusing steroids. Testifying before Congress in 2005, Dr. Harrison Pope, a professor of psychiatry at McLean Hospital at Harvard Medical School, said that the more accurate number of women abusing an anabolic steroid would be 1 in 500.

Part of the reason for the increase in steroid abuse among girls and women is their increased participation in organized sports. Fewer programs, and fewer dollars supporting those programs, can make competition to make the team very intense. Just as some male athletes have done, some female athletes have turned to steroids and similar substances to increase their chances of success. And they have their steroid-troubled role models as well. Track standouts Kelli White and Marion Jones have allegedly been involved in steroid abuse.

Most females who abuse steroids, however, do not do so to gain an athletic edge; they are most interested in the drugs' ability to reduce body fat and increase muscles. Many of them have a *concurrent* eating disorder or a psychiatric condition such as muscle or body dysmorphia.

How Steroids Are Abused

Steroids are versatile when it comes to how they can be taken into the body. Today, there are ten major classes of anabolic steroids based on how they are taken into the body and the carrier **solvent** that introduces the steroid into the body. The classes are:

1. oral
2. injectable oil based
3. injectable water based
4. **transdermal** patch or gel
5. aerosol, propellant-based preparation
6. **sublingual**

The Olympic flame has inspired great achievement and courage; unfortunately, it has also inspired some to abuse steroids.

Undetectable, That's What You Are . . . or Are You?

One thing can be said about manufacturers of steroids and performance-enhancing supplements—they can be sneaky.

Once the Olympics and other sports bodies decided to test for steroids and other substances, the race was on to find something that couldn't be detected by tests as they are now conducted. Enter tetrahydrogestrinone, better known as THG. Exactly who discovered THG is not known, but rumors abound that it's a product of BALCO.

THG is a designer steroid. Its makeup is slightly chemically altered from two steroids tested for and banned by the International Olympic Committee and other sports governing bodies. Originally marketed as a dietary supplement, THG did not meet the definition of such established by the FDA. This government agency has ruled that THG is an unapproved new drug, making it illegal to market in the United States.

7. homemade transdermal preparation
8. androgen-estrogen combination
9. counterfeit anabolic steroid
10. over the counter

Of the most popular steroids, Anadrol® (oxymetholone) and Oxandrin® (oxandrolone) are available in pill or capsule form. Steroids such as Dec-Durabolin® (nandrolone decanoate) and Equipoise® (boldenone undecylenate) are injected into muscle. Other forms of steroids can be taken through transdermal gels and creams.

Despite their known dangers—and the fact that they are controlled substances—obtaining steroids can be relatively easy. The media is full of stories of coaches, trainers, even parents who have supplied young athletes with steroids. Some neighborhood gyms may look more like a pharmacy with all of the steroids and other supplements that suppliers have available for their clients. The Internet is another source for steroids and supplements. A Google search conducted in March 2012, for "buy anabolic steroids" returned more than 345,000 hits.

Dosing Patterns

Most individuals who abuse steroids have a very distinct pattern to their usage. Many use a "cycling" pattern, which involves taking steroids over a specific period, stopping for a while, and then starting the process over again. The periods on and off the steroids vary from days to weeks to months.

"Stacking" is another popular way of taking steroids. This pattern involves taking several different steroids, usually mixing ingestible and injectable types of the drugs. In some cases, individuals even use steroids developed for use in veterinary medicine. Individuals who stack their steroids believe that the mixing of the steroids increase their ultimate effect; they'll get better results than if they had used the individual steroids alone. There is no scientific proof that this is the case.

When abusers "pyramid," they slowly increase how much or how often (or both) they take steroids; many also include stacking in their pyramid routine. They often operate on a cycle of six to twelve weeks. At first, the dosage is low. Gradually, dosage and frequency increase, until they reach a peak during the midpoint of the cycle. Abusers then start tapering off the dosage until they are no longer taking steroids. When this point is reached, individuals usually spend some time completely off steroids before resuming another pyramid cycle. The theory behind pyramiding is that the gradual increase in dosage allows the body to adapt to the high doses. The steroid-free period allows the body to recuperate before

In some cases, unscrupulous coaches have supplied young adults with illegal steroids.

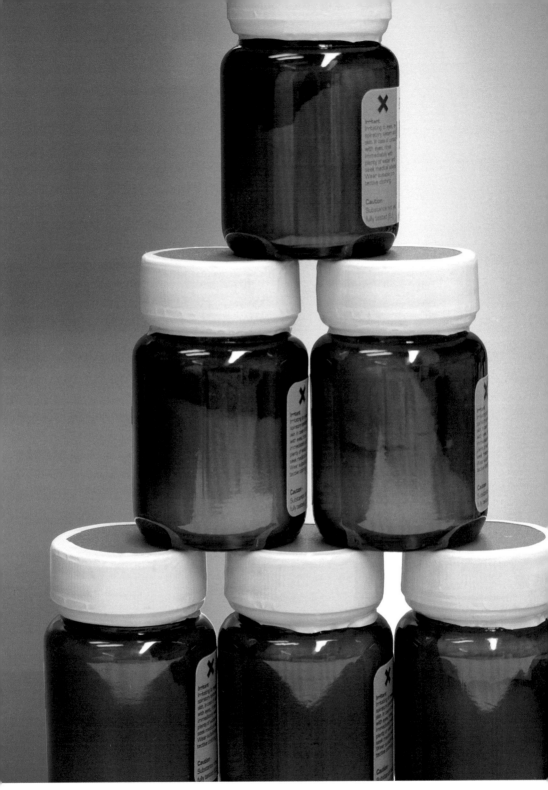

"Stacking" and "pyramiding" are two popular patterns for abusing steroids.

the process is begun again. No scientific proof indicates that this way of taking steroids has any added benefits, or that it is a "safer" way to abuse steroids.

As important as knowing why someone starts using steroids—and how they are getting and abusing them—is knowing the short-term and long-term effects these substances have on the body.

Lance Armstrong—Hero?

His name is synonymous with courage and success—and controversy. No name is better known in the world of bicycle racing than Lance Armstrong. He began his athletic career as a triathlete, but by age seventeen had decided to concentrate on bicycle racing. It didn't take long before he began to dominate the sport, and his dominance would lead to controversy that would shadow him throughout his cycling career. His outstanding success in the arduous Tour de France was unprecedented and, to some, unbelievable. Lance has often been the subject of accusations that he took performance-enhancing drugs to help him win an unprecedented seven consecutive Tour de France competitions. None of the allegations were proven, and for most fans, Lance's image remains untarnished. In 1996, few would have thought that Lance would reach such heights.

On October 2, 1996, the native Texan was diagnosed with testicular cancer—the most common cancer in males between the ages of fifteen and thirty-five. But, the cancer was not confined to a testicle; it had already spread to Lance's lungs and brain. His doctors told him that his chances of beating the cancer were 40 percent. (After Lance had recovered, one of his doctors told him that the 40 percent figure was only meant to give him hope; his actual chance of survival was as little as 3 percent.) His treatment was successful, and as soon as his cancer went into remission, Lance returned to training. In 1998, he was again racing professionally.

After he won his battle with cancer, Lance established the Lance Armstrong Foundation. The Wear Yellow Live Strong program supports people with cancer and survivors and provides educational programs to increase cancer awareness. Their biggest fundraiser is the yellow Livestrong wristband. Tens of millions of wristbands have been sold worldwide. Athletic wear company Nike also launched a line of shoes carrying the "Live Strong" yellow in support of the foundation and its projects.

In 2005, Lance announced that he was retiring. It wasn't a permanent retirement though, and he later announced that he was reentering the world of competitive racing in 2008. He rode in the Tour de France the following two years, although he did not win. Then, in 2011, he announced for a second time that he was ending his racing career. This time it looks like it's for good.

Lance has retired from professional bicycling, but not sports. In November 2006, he ran in the ING New York City Marathon. He finished in under three hours, which he had set as his goal. He later went on to run it again, and also ran the Boston Marathon. Lance remains a tireless worker on behalf of cancer awareness as well. He is a frequent visitor to hospitals to visit people with cancer and is a popular and effective speaker on the subject.

His retirement has not meant an end to speculation that he had some added help in his racing success, either. The admission by former members of his racing team that they had used performance-enhancing drugs caused many to wonder if Lance Armstrong was really one of the few in the highest caliber of bicycle racing to be immune to taking illegal substances.

3 What Are the Risks?

At 6-foot-2, most people would consider 18-year-old Chris Walsh a big guy. But the athlete from Plano, Texas, once believed he wasn't big enough.

So he started using steroids at age 15. "I just wanted to get bigger," Chris says.

He did get bigger—and meaner.

"I got angry. Always wanted to fight, always hitting things." . . .

[Chris's mother] thought her son needed anger management. He thought he needed more of the illegal drug from a supplier at a gym.

"It was almost like I was a heroin addict," Chris says. "It got to the point where I needed the injection to work out, to feel good about myself."

(*Source*: "Teens and Steroids: A Dangerous Mix." CBS News, June 3, 2004)

Anger is just one of the possible side effects of taking steroids. Some potential side effects are relatively minor: acne, oily hair, purple or red spots on the body, legs and feet swelling, and bad breath. The user's appetite may increase, and bone marrow may become stimulated into producing more red blood cells. Many find that their libido increases as well, though performance ability may not.

Other potential side effects are far more serious and include the possibility of death. Fortunately, most adverse side effects are reversible once the steroid use stops.

Just as statistical evidence on steroid abuse is lacking, so are formal studies on their long-term serious effects. Information about potential side effects comes from anecdotal or animal research evidence rather than formal studies. Because of this, potentially serious side effects may be underreported. The NIDA has also expressed concern about the underreporting of potentially serious side effects because they can take a long time to surface.

Male-pattern baldness is one of the irreversible effects of taking steroids.

In a study cited by the NIDA in their 2006 report, mice that received over one-fifth of their lifetime steroid doses (comparable to those taken by human athletes) had a high rate of early death.

Though death is a potential side effect, there are many others. Steroids appear to affect all areas of the human body.

Endocrine System

Because of the makeup of steroids (see chapter 1), their abuse obviously affects the production of hormones. Some of these changes can be reversed when steroid use ends. In men, these reversible changes include decreased sperm production and testicular atrophy—the shrinking of the size of the testicles. In other cases, changes can't be reversed; once they occur, they become a part of life, unless other measures are taken. Irreversible effects in males include male-pattern baldness and gynecomastia—the increased size of breasts.

In women, the effects are different. Remember that anabolic steroids are similar to testosterone, the male sex hormone. While the increased testosterone in men can make them develop female characteristics, in women, it causes the development of male characteristics such as decreased breast size. Women's skin can become rougher. Though women may also develop baldness, hair on other parts of their bodies may increase, becoming coarser and more dense. *Clitoral hypertrophy* may occur. Women's voices deepen, sometimes significantly. Most of these side effects are reversible once a woman stops taking steroids.

Musculoskeletal System

During puberty and adolescence individuals reach their adult height. Sex hormones, such as testosterone, tell the body when the growth is to begin and when it is to end. If a child or adolescent takes an anabolic steroid,

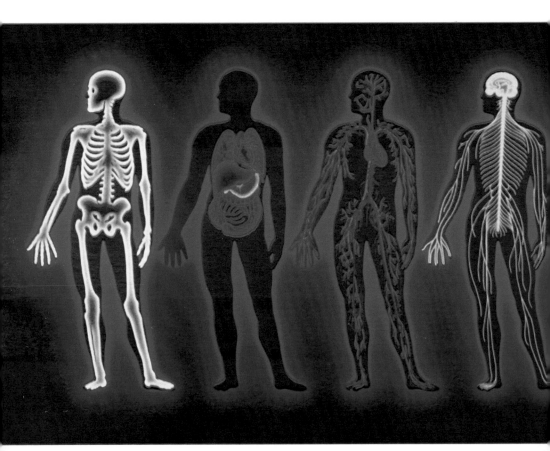

Taking steroids affects many of the body's systems, including the muscles; bones; heart, blood, and lungs; nerves; and many of the organs.

the level of testosterone in the body is artificially high. Put simply, the steroid-increased testosterone level tells the body's inner workings it's time to stop growing; you're tall enough. When this happens, the bones stop growing. If the body receives this message from steroid abuse, the individual does not reach his full height.

In some cases, however, under the careful monitoring of a health-care professional, steroids can actually cause height to increase. You can read more about one case in a sidebar in chapter 1.

Cardiovascular System

You won't have much energy if your cardiovascular system is impaired, and abuse of steroids have a proven track record of affecting cardiovascular efficacy. Heart attacks and strokes have felled steroid-using athletes under thirty years of age. Steroid use can result in elevated blood pressure, another risk factor for heart attack and stroke. Researchers have found that steroids contribute to cardiovascular disease by affecting lipoproteins, which carry *cholesterol* throughout the body.

There are two types of cholesterol: low-density lipoprotein (LDL) and high-density lipoprotein (HDL). Low LDL and high HDL are important to cardiovascular health. Taking steroids (and oral steroids seem to be the biggest problem) leads to high LDL and low HDL, which allows fatty substances to attach themselves as plaque to the inside walls of the arteries. If the buildup of the plaque continues, the heart will not be able to receive a sufficient supply of blood through the arteries. This is a heart attack waiting to happen.

Steroid use also increases the possibility of blood clots forming in the blood vessels. These clots can stop the flow of blood to the heart. The heart can be damaged by this disruption and its ability to work efficiently be adversely affected.

Liver

The effects of steroid abuse on the liver can be deadly. Liver tumors and a rare condition called peliosis hepatis have been found in people with a history of steroid abuse. In peliosis hepatis, cysts filled with blood form in the liver. Should liver tumors or the cysts of peliosis hepatis rupture, internal bleeding will occur. Left unchecked, or found too late, these hemorrhages may even cause the individual to bleed to death.

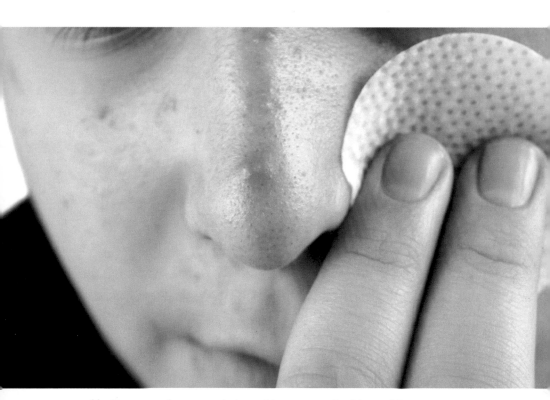

Most teenagers have acne, but steroid use can make this condition worse.

Male-Specific Side Effects

- gynecomastia
- reduced sexual function and temporary infertility
- testicular atrophy
- pain when urinating

Female-Specific Side Effects

- increase in body hair, though scalp hair may be lost
- deepening of the voice
- clitoral hypertrophy
- temporary decrease in menstrual cycles

Adolescent-Specific Side Effects

- stunted growth
- accelerated bone maturation
- slight beard growth

Street Names

- roids
- juice
- hype
- pump

Signs of Steroid Use

- quick weight and muscle gains (when used in a weight training program)
- aggressiveness and combativeness
- jaundice
- purple or red spots on the body
- swelling of feet and lower legs
- trembling
- unexplained darkening of the skin
- persistent unpleasant breath odor
- severe acne breakouts and oily skin

(*Source*: Focus Adolescent Services. www.focusas.com/Steroids.html)

Steroids, HIV/AIDS, and Other Infections

Choosing to inject steroids brings with it the very high risk of developing diseases such as AIDS or hepatitis B and C, all potentially deadly illnesses. Exposure to HIV (the virus that causes AIDS) and to hepatitis generally comes when someone uses an unclean needle to inject the steroid. However, that is not the only way to contract such infections. Sometimes, drugs such as steroids are not produced in the pristine pharmaceutical plants we might expect. Drugs, especially those often abused, can be pro-

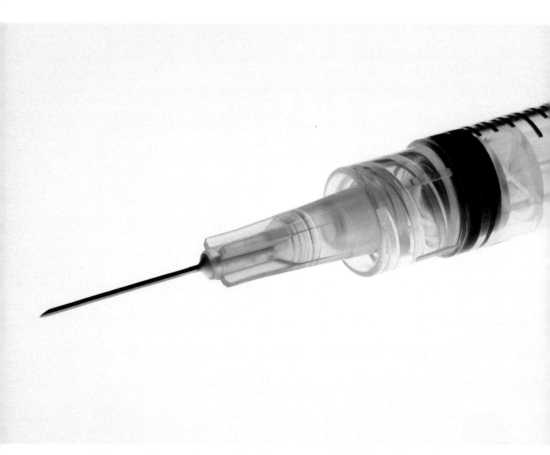

When steroid users share needles, they may spread HIV, hepatitis, or other diseases.

The Legacy of Taylor Hooton

Taylor Hooton was popular, happy, and loved baseball and was good at it. But he committed suicide just a month after his seventeenth birthday, just before the start of his senior year in high school. Were it not for his family and the Taylor Hooton Foundation, his story might have ended there: just another drug-abusing teenager who met a tragic end. His family, however, wouldn't let Taylor's life be for nothing.

After their son died, Taylor's parents learned that he had low self-esteem. He felt that to be as good as anyone else, he had to be bigger. One of his coaches had also recommended that Taylor do what he needed to get bigger for baseball.

Besides gaining thirty pounds—mostly muscle—other things happened to Taylor while he was on steroids. He stole from his parents, he threw a phone at the wall, he beat up his girlfriend's old boyfriend, he stole a camera and a computer while on vacation, he flew into intense rages that were followed by seemingly sincere apologies.

Finally, Taylor's family had had enough. He was tested for drugs, but the test was only for recreational drugs and came back clean. When the family returned from a vacation to England, they confronted Taylor, telling him his behavior was unacceptable and that he had to get his act together. His parents grounded him. The following morning, Taylor tried to convince his mother to change her mind, but she refused. Taylor went upstairs to his room, made a noose from his belts, and hanged himself from the door of his bedroom. In Taylor's room, his father and law enforcement officers found vials of steroids as well as needles and syringes.

After Taylor's death, his parents formed the Taylor Hooton Foundation. His father, Don, travels around the country talking about steroid use in high schools. The foundation's goal is to prevent another needless death by educating parents, school officials, and coaches about the dangers of steroids.

duced under less than sanitary conditions. Contaminates can enter the drugs, and infections such as endocarditis, a potentially fatal inflammation of the heart, can spread unchecked.

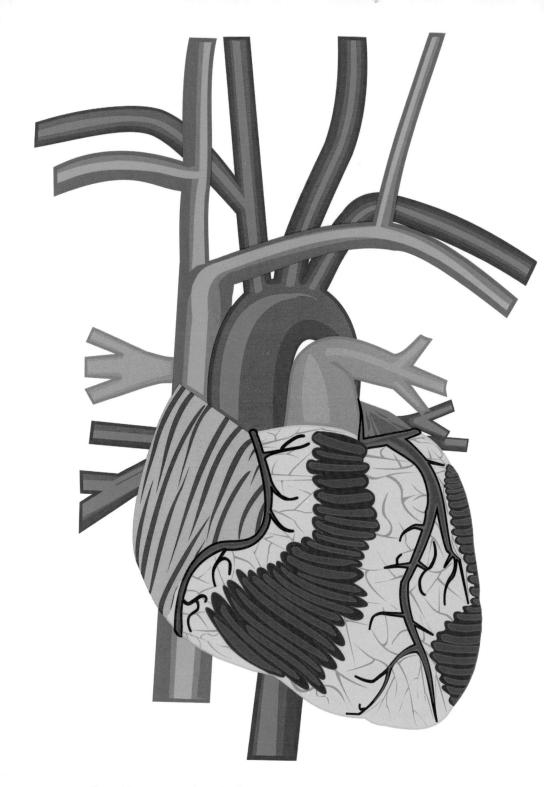

If steroids are contaminated, infection can enter the bloodstream; endocarditis, an inflammation of the heart, is a possibly fatal result.

Commonly Abused Steroids

Oral Steroids	Injectable Steroids
Anadrol (oxymetholone)	Deca-Durabolin (nandrolone decanoate)
Oxandrin (oxandrolone)	Durabolin (nandrolone phenpropionate)
Dianabol (methandrostenolone)	Depo-Testosterone (testosterone cypionate)
Winstrol (stanozolol)	Equipose (boldenone undecylenate)
Tetrahydrogestrinone (THG)	

Steroids and Behavior

Chris Walsh, whose story opens this chapter, experienced just one of the behavioral effects that steroids seem to cause—increased aggression or "roid rage." Both research studies and anecdotal evidence show that, when taken in high doses, steroids can increase aggression. According to the NIDA (2006), some individuals who abuse steroids reported that they committed physical violence, robbery, theft, vandalism, or burglary. Most reported that they were more apt to commit these crimes when they were taking steroids. Many researchers believe that the problems with mood or behavior occur because of changes in hormones.

Although a few formal studies have been done on the relationship between steroid use and aggression, no definitive findings have been reached, because the results in the studies have varied, even within the studies. In some studies, there is no or only slight differences between the results found in individuals using steroids and others using placebos. In other studies, however, a definite relationship shows up between taking steroids and increased aggression. Since the results are contradictory, this is an area that requires further research and studies with a larger population base.

Increased aggression may be the most publicized behavioral side effect of steroid abuse, but it isn't the only

Steroids can cause out-of-control feelings of rage. Some people "treat" this condition by taking heroin and other illegal drugs.

one. **Mania**, **delusions**, and depression have also been reported in individuals who abuse steroids.

Another behavioral side effect of abusing steroids is codependence on another drug. In many cases, the additional drug is taken to alleviate some of the potential adverse effects of the steroids. A NIDA (2006) study of 227 men undergoing inpatient treatment in 1999 for heroin or other opioid abuse found that 9.3 percent of them had started their illicit drug use by abusing anabolic steroids. Of those, 86 percent had used the opioids to "treat" the insomnia and rage they had as a side effect of taking steroids.

For some individuals, no matter how bad the side effects are or how dire the outlook caused by their steroid abuse, they just won't—or can't—stop. For others, a time will come when they say enough is enough, and they begin the journey to a steroid-free life.

4 Treatment For Steroid Abuse

Taylor Hooton was a classmate [of Chris's] and a gifted athlete who committed suicide last July. He went into a deep depression while withdrawing from steroids.

"When Taylor died, it was a huge wake-up call," Chris says. . . .

"I was like coming down from the high just like any other drug, and started getting really depressed," Chris says.

He abruptly stopped using steroids after Taylor Hooton died.

"I'd just be, like, how bad is today going to be, you know? Could today be any worse than yesterday? And it always was."

He even thought about taking his own life. Several times he drove to an overpass, where he thought, "If I just jumped, it'd be the easy way out."

(*Source:* "Teens and Steroids: A Dangerous Mix." CBS News, June 3, 2004)

The story Chris tells is not unique. First, Taylor and he both be-came depressed when withdrawing from steroids. Second, sometimes it

Scientific Definitions

Talking about addiction and dependence can be confusing, because different people use the words to mean different things. According to most scientists: *addiction is a primary, chronic, neurobiological disease, with genetic, psychosocial, and environmental factors influencing its development and manifestations. It is characterized by behaviors that include one or more of the following:*

- *impaired control over drug use*
- *compulsive use*
- *continued use despite harm, and craving.*

The American Psychiatric Association (APA) and the World Health Organization (WHO) use the word "dependence" for the same concept. A more common definition for physical dependence, however, is this:

A state of adaptation that is manifested by a drug class specific withdrawal syndrome that can be produced by abrupt cessation, rapid dose reduction, decreasing blood level of drug and/or administration of an antagonist and is relieved by the readministration of the drug or another drug of the same pharmacologic class.

takes something really big to make one "see the light" and change his ways, ultimately finding a way out of addiction.

What Is Addiction?

Sometimes the language used to describe aspects of illicit and misused drugs can be confusing. This can be true when discussing dependence and addiction. Dependence can be either psychological or physical. When a person is physically dependent on a chemical substance, that means if she were to stop taking the drug suddenly, her body will have a predictable physiologic response, such as headaches or agitation. A person who is psychologically dependent relies emotionally on a particular drug. In either case, the person is not truly addicted, however.

Addiction is a far more serious condition. It is a chronic, neurobiological disease, whose development and symptoms are influenced by genetic, psychosocial, and environmental factors. Addiction is characterized by behaviors that include one or more of the following:

- impaired control over drug use
- compulsive use
- continued use despite harm
- craving

Abused but Addictive?

Without a doubt, many people abuse steroids. There has even been observations of what appear to resemble withdrawal symptoms when some people discontinue their use. Whether these drugs can be considered truly addicting, however, in the sense that cocaine, heroin, alcohol, and nicotine can cause addiction is not clear. For example, the American Psychiatric Association, which develops widely accepted criteria for dependence and withdrawal, does not recognize a category of dependence designated steroid dependence or withdrawal as a medical disorder. It does, however, allow that the infrequent fraction of users that appear to meet criteria for withdrawal be lumped under "Other."

Furthermore, as observed by the former chief of the laboratory of the National Institute on Drug Abuse charged with testing drugs for addictiveness ("abuse liability"), Dr. Jack Henningfield, steroids do not produce

The Words the Experts Use

Abuse: The use of a drug in a manner detrimental to the individual or society but not meeting criteria for addiction or dependence. Abuse is sometimes used as a synonym for drug abuse, substance abuse, drug addiction, chemical dependency, and substance dependency.

Diversion: The removal of legitimately manufactured controlled medications from lawful, legitimate use into illicit drug trafficking. Diversion cases involve, but are not limited to, physicians who sell prescriptions to drug dealers or abusers; pharmacists who falsify records and subsequently sell the medications; employees who steal from inventory; executives who falsify orders to cover illicit sales; prescription forgers; and individuals who commit armed robbery of pharmacies and drug distributors.

Misuse: The exposure resulting from 1) the use of a prescription medication in ways other than how it was prescribed, or 2) the use of an over-the-counter medication contrary to approved labeling unless taken as directed by a healthcare provider, and below the threshold of abuse.

Nonmedical use: The use of a prescription medication in a manner inconsistent with accepted medical practice, or the use of an over-the-counter medication contrary to approved labeling.

Recovery: A process of overcoming both physical and psychological dependence on a psychoactive substance, with a commitment to a drug free state. This is frequently referred to as a commitment to "sobriety," emphasizing the fact that the terminology has its roots more in alcohol treatment, which stresses the life-long nature of the process.

Tolerance: Tolerance is a state of adaptation in which exposure to a drug induces changes that result in a diminution of one or more of the drug's effects over time. It creates a need for markedly increased amounts of the drug to achieve intoxication or desired effects, or markedly diminished effects with continued use of the same amount of the drug.

Withdrawal: A constellation of symptoms that can follow rapid discontinuation of daily use of most addictive drugs with symptoms differing across drugs but frequently including withdrawal or a tendency to resume drug taking. Withdrawal can occur in people who do not show other signs of addiction, such as pain patients on opioids who stop taking their medicines, or babies born by addicted mothers.

the effects of classically addicting drugs. These effects include quick onsetting psychoactive effects such as getting "high" and serving as rewards for animals, nor do they produce tolerance to these psychoactive effects with continued use. This does not reduce the seriousness of concerns about their abuse; after all, no one thinks poison is addictive, but it is still dangerous! Used inappropriately, steroids can poison the body and produce severe harmful effects, including death, as described earlier.

All this posed a dilemma for the National Institute on Drug Abuse, Drug Enforcement Administration, and Food and Drug Administration, which make recommendations for designating drugs as controlled substances on the basis of the official criteria of the Controlled Substances Act. Because steroids did not clearly meet the criteria but were unquestionably being abused to serious harmful effect, the U.S. Congress stepped in and designated steroids as controlled substances in 1990.

Symptoms that have been observed in some people that might constitute a withdrawal syndrome include the following:

- drastic mood swings
- fatigue
- restlessness
- loss of appetite
- insomnia
- decreased libido
- cravings for steroids
- depression

The most serious symptom is depression. In some cases, it leads to suicidal thoughts (as in Chris's case), while in others it leads to actual suicide attempts and even successes, as with Taylor Hooton. Some studies have shown that, left untreated, some symptoms of depression can linger for more than a year after the person has stopped taking steroids.

A Series of Steps

Like many areas of steroid abuse research, few studies have researched the treatment of steroid abuse. Most of the data are provided by physicians and others who treat steroid addiction rather than from formal studies. In many ways, however, overcoming steroid addiction is the same as with every other form of addiction. The first step is to admit there is a problem, that one is an addict. In some ways, this may be the hardest step; the journey to sobriety can never be completed without taking that first step of admitting to being an addict.

The most effective method of addiction treatment involves a multidisciplinary approach—and it doesn't happen over night.

Detoxification

When one decides to break free from most addictions, the body must go through a process of withdrawal to rid itself of the toxic substances of the drug. In the case of steroid abuse, this detoxification process is generally not as intensive as it is with other drugs. However, the individual will go through a period in which he experiences some or all of the withdrawal symptoms listed earlier in this chapter. How long withdrawal lasts depends on how much and what type of steroid was taken, as well as the length of time the person has been abusing steroids. If the withdrawal symptoms are severe or long-lasting, the process may take place in a hospital or other treatment facility.

For some, this process might be enough to prevent further abuse. For others, however, follow-up treatment is beneficial; studies have shown that most people with addictions will return to their previous behaviors if treatment ends with only detoxification.

Two primary methods are used to treat addiction: behavioral and *pharmacological*.

Breaking free from addiction requires that a person climb a series of steps; the first is always to admit that the problem exists.

Behavioral Treatment Programs

Put simply, behavioral treatment programs teach people with addictions to change their behaviors so they are less likely to repeat those that led to addiction in the first place. Unfortunately, nothing about addiction is simple. Though behavioral treatment programs do help those with addictions find ways to avoid behaviors that can cause a relapse, they also need to help them discover what led to those behaviors initially. Cognitive-behavioral therapy helps the individuals recognize how thought patterns influence behaviors. With therapy, individuals learn how to change negative thought patterns, thereby changing behaviors. Individual and family therapy can help the person with addiction and those around her learn how to live with and as a recovering addict. Therapy can also help the addicted individual and her associates handle *relapses*; most people do relapse at some point during recovery.

Behavioral treatment programs also help those with addictions handle life without the effects they had from steroids. If the individual is an athlete and still participates in sports, he must learn how to be around others who may be abusing steroids. He may also need to learn how to live with a new body. The best treatment results are achieved when the individual practices *abstinence* from any use of steroids. If the individual achieved a significant increase in muscle mass, he may be unable to maintain that level without the use of steroids. Though he can exercise and lift weights to retain some body mass, he's unlikely to retain the bulk he achieved artificially. To be successful, he'll have to learn how to handle temptations and the cravings he may experience, even those brought on by the desire to have what once was.

Once a person is no longer taking steroids, he may not be able to maintain the muscle mass he had achieved while using the chemical. To break free of his addiction, he will need to be believe that total good health is more important than physical appearance.

Steroids—Pumped Up and Dangerous 77

Generally, behavioral treatment programs begin with a period of inpatient treatment, though this might not be necessary for the person addicted to steroids. Depending on the length, severity, and drug of addiction, inpatient treatment can be short-term (usually a minimum of thirty days) or long-term residential. At first, some programs allow inpatients to have minimal—if any—contact with the "outside world." Patients concentrate on learning about themselves and their relationship with the drug. Later, family and perhaps close friends are encouraged to participate in the treatment program.

Depression may be one of the side effects of steroid withdrawal. Although medication cannot "cure" the addiction, antidepressants can help individuals deal with this troublesome symptom.

Pharmacological Treatment Programs

Many medications used to treat steroid withdrawal restore the hormonal imbalance the steroids have caused. Other medications are used to treat specific withdrawal symptoms such as headaches and muscle and joint pain. Special attention will be paid to any symptoms of depression. Should the individual exhibit symptoms of depression, antidepressants may be prescribed, along with other forms of therapy. Of course, if long-term damage has been done to the individual's body, medications and other treatments will be provided. Unlike addiction to other drugs, there are no pharmacological treatments for steroid addiction itself.

Most treatment programs use a combination of behavioral treatment and pharmacological methods. Individuals are also encouraged to supplement their programs with support groups such as Narcotics Anonymous.

Narcotics Anonymous

The recovering abuser of steroids may find success by using detox alone or with a combination of behavioral and pharmacological therapies. However, support groups such as Narcotics Anonymous (NA) help many. Based on the successful Alcoholics Anonymous (AA) program, the first NA meetings were held in the early 1950s in Los Angeles, California. As found on its website (www. na.org), the organization described itself this way in its first publication:

> NA is a nonprofit fellowship or society of men and women for whom drugs had become a major

problem. We . . . meet regularly to help each other stay clean. . . . We are not interested in what or how much you used . . . but only in what you want to do about your problem and how we can help.

In the more than fifty years since, NA has grown into one of the largest organizations of its kind. Today, groups are located all over the world, and its books and pamphlets are published in thirty-two languages. No matter where the group is located, each chapter is based on the twelve steps first formulated in AA:

The Twelve Steps of NA

1. We admitted we were powerless over drugs—that our lives had become unmanageable.
2. Came to believe that a Power greater than ourselves could restore us to sanity.
3. Made a decision to turn our will and our lives over to the care of God as we understand Him.
4. Made a searching and fearless moral inventory of ourselves.
5. Admitted to God, and to our selves, and to another human being the exact nature of our wrongs.
6. We're entirely ready to have God remove all these defects of character.
7. Humbly asked Him to remove our shortcomings.
8. Made a list of all persons we had harmed, and became willing to make amends to them all.
9. Made direct amends to such people wherever possible, except when to do so would injure them or others.
10. Continued to take personal inventory and when we were wrong promptly admitted it.

Freedom from steroids can be difficult to achieve—but ultimately, it can be more exhilarating than the muscle mass and physical strength these chemicals offered.

11. Sought through prayer and meditation to improve our conscious contact with God as we understand Him, praying only for knowledge of His will for us and the power to carry that out.
12. Having had a spiritual awakening as the result of these steps, we tried to carry this message to drug addicts and to practice these principles in all our affairs.

Other Support Groups

A support group exists for almost every imaginable subject. And why is that so? Sure, some people just like to **commiserate** with others who share the same problem, but the fact of the matter is that these groups work for many people. Sometimes commiseration is a good thing. It can help an individual feel better to know she isn't the only person facing a particular difficulty. Individuals can

Taking time for solitude, prayer, or meditation is an important part of NA's approach to addiction treatment.

learn different ways to deal with situations or even health issues.

Educational facilities, hospitals or treatment centers, or religious institutions sponsor support groups. Other groups seem to form *serendipitously*, without the official sponsorship of an organization. Most don't have as strict rules about anonymity as NA or AA follows, but every member's privacy should be respected by all connected with the group.

Not all people are comfortable sharing things about themselves in group settings, face to face. For them, the Internet offers a wide variety of chat rooms and e-mail lists. Even though this isn't an in-person meeting, individuals should be very careful about how much personal information they share, including last names, addresses, and telephone numbers. Sadly, not everyone on the Internet is who they say they are, and reasonable caution is called for.

Regardless of whether someone participates in an in-person support group or in an online chat, all advice—especially medical advice—should be taken cautiously. Consider the source. Is the person a medical professional? Is the information from a reliable source? If looking at Web sites, make sure you know who is responsible for the information placed there. Often it is a pharmaceutical manufacturer touting the wonders of its medication on a slickly produced site that gives few clues to the writer's motives. Government sites are generally good sources for reliable information.

And remember—what works for one person doesn't always work for another. Before trying anything new, check it out thoroughly with the appropriate people, such as a health-care professional.

What Do Rehab Programs Accomplish?

A professional who has experience in dealing with substance-related disorders must always monitor treatment that includes psychiatric medication. The goal of treatment for substance-related disorders is to end the individual's dependence on the substance and to restore her ability to function appropriately in society. While it is not always possible to achieve 100 percent abstinence from an addictive substance, a reduction in use coupled with an ability to carry out family duties and employment roles is evidence of improvement.

Abstinence

In many cases it seems that as long as the substance is in the blood stream, thinking remains distorted. Often during the first days or weeks of total abstinence, we see a gradual clearing of thinking processes. This is a complex psychological and biological phenomenon, and is one of the elements that inpatient programs are able to provide by making sure the patient is fully detoxified and remains abstinent during his or her stay.

Removal of Denial

In some cases, when someone other than the patient, such as a parent, employer, or other authority, is convinced there is a problem, but the addict is not yet sure, voluntary attendance at a rehab program will provide enough clarification to remove this basic denial. Even those who are convinced they have a problem with substances usually don't admit to themselves or others the full extent of the addiction. Rehab uses group process to identify and help the individual to let go of these expectable forms of denial.

Removal of Isolation

As addictions progress, relationships deteriorate in quality. However, the bonds between fellow recovering people are widely recognized as one of the few forces powerful enough to keep recovery on track. The rehab experience, whether it is inpatient or outpatient involves in-depth sharing in a group setting. This kind of sharing creates strong interpersonal bonds among group members. These bonds help to form a support system that will be powerful enough to sustain the individual during the first months of abstinence.

"Basic Training"

Basic training is a good way to think of the experience of rehab. Soldiers need a rapid course to give them the basic knowledge and skills they will need to fight in a war. Some kinds of learning need to be practiced so well that you can do them without thinking. In addition to the learning, trainees become physically fit, and perhaps most important, form emotional bonds that help keep up morale when the going is hard.

(*Source*: Partnership for a Drug-Free America)

5 Legal Consequences of Steroid Abuse

His is a name synonymous with baseball—Barry Bonds, son of a Hall-of-Famer and destined to become one himself. Or is he?

As the 2006 baseball season came to a close, Bonds had surpassed the number of home runs hit by the legendary Babe Ruth and was zeroing in on Hank Aaron's all-time home-run record. Instead of media attention for those admirable feats, Bond's name most often appeared in the paper—and not just on the sports' page—for his possible involvement in one of the biggest scandals to hit professional sports.

Burlingame, California, is the home of an unassuming-looking sports nutrition center named the Bay Area Laboratory Co-operative, better known these days as BALCO. The center has long been the subject of an investigation into accusations that they had provided steroids and other performance-enhancing substances to many athletes, including Barry Bonds. But he is far from the only one. Others rumored to have received substances from BALCO include track star Marion Jones, baseball players Jason Giambi, Benito Santiago, and Gary Sheffield, and professional

Since 1988, Congress has been involved in the relationship between sports and steroids.

football players Bill Romanowski, Tyrone Wheatley, and Barrett Robbins.

Bonds eventually got in trouble for lying under oath about using steroids, since he continued to deny that he knowingly took steroids or any performance-enhancing substances. The jury eventually decided he did.

In 2011, Bonds was sentenced to 30 days of house arrest, two years probation and 250 hours of community service. His baseball career is over, destroyed by his legal troubles.

It took a while for steroids to gain popularity in the United States. Then it took a while longer for the government to determine that the possibility of abuse and addiction outweighed the medical benefits they had. In 1990, anabolic steroids were placed on the controlled substances list, placing restrictions on their manufacture, distribution, possession, and use. It is illegal to possess or sell anabolic steroids in all fifty states.

The Law, Anabolic Steroids, and Athletes

The 2006 congressional hearings about sports and anabolic steroids were not the first. In fact, from 1988 to 1990, Congress bowed to increasing media coverage of the relationship between sports and steroids and held hearings to investigate their dangers. The result of those hearings was the inclusion of anabolic steroids on the controlled substance list. Incidentally, most of the experts who testified before these hearings were against adding steroids to the list.

The Anabolic Steroids Control Act of 1990 applies to every federal court in the United States. As a Schedule III drug, under federal law, simple possession (which does not include the intent to sell) can be punished by up to one year in jail, a minimum fine of $1,000, or both. If the person convicted of simple possession has a previous arrest and conviction for specified crimes, including any crimes involving drugs or narcotics, they must be imprisoned for at least fifteen days (but the sentence can be up to two years) and receive a minimum fine of $2,500. If the Schedule III–offender has two or more such prior convictions, he must spend a minimum of ninety days and a maximum of three years in jail. He is also subject to a minimum fine of $5,000.

Those can be some pretty stiff sentences just for *having* some anabolic steroids. But, the person who sells or possesses with the intent to sell has some serious prob-

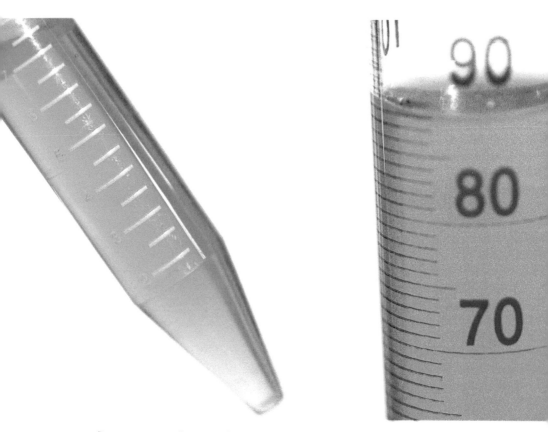

Drug testing can be a significant expense for public schools that are already facing serious financial challenges.

Steroids in the Locker Room

While the actual number of high school athletes who use steroids is not known with certainty, steroid use has become a problem on high school campuses across the country. Some schools have resorted to random drug testing of athletes in an effort to fight the problem. Though it might help fight the problem of steroid abuse, it has left schools open to other problems.

Financial resources at most schools have been cut drastically over the past few years. Athletic programs, music and art programs, and after-school programs are just some of the areas facing budget cuts. This also means the money may not be there to conduct drug tests. One small school estimates that the cost of testing for steroid use would be more than $44,000. That's a figure that many schools would find difficult—if not impossible—to come up with.

Another question surrounding random drug testing is constitutional, not financial. Is there just cause to test for drugs if an individual has not shown evidence of using them? And who should be tested? Is it all right to test just athletes, or should everyone who participates in an extracurricular activity—a member of the debate team or choir even—be tested? Where does the right to privacy enter into the equation?

So far, there are a lot of questions and very few answers. Chances are no solutions are on the near horizon, so the discussion—and steroid use—will continue.

lems. This is a felony offense, punishable by up to five years in prison and a $250,000 fine! After release from prison, the former inmate is on parole for at least two years. If the person has a prior drug or narcotic conviction, she can expect to spend a maximum of ten years in prison, followed by at least four years on parole, as well as pay a higher fine. The federal government takes anabolic steroids very seriously.

State Laws and Anabolic Steroids

After the U.S. federal law went into affect, most states quickly amended their laws to conform to the federal laws. While the federal law is uniform across the country, the same cannot be said about state laws. Not every state classifies steroids at the same level. In some states, such as Delaware, Michigan, and Tennessee, it's not only the users being targeted. These states have rules regarding the prescribing of anabolic steroids and strongly caution health-care providers, including doctors and pharmacists, not to give out anabolic steroids for nonmedical use.

In New York State, possession of any amount of anabolic steroids is prosecuted as a Class A misdemeanor punishable by a maximum of one year in jail. Sell any amount of anabolic steroids in New York State and the person has committed a Class D felony, calling for a sentence of up to seven years in prison. New York State has a rather broad definition of the word "sell." Even if the person gives away the anabolic steroids, he can be charged with selling.

Targeting Steroids

While law enforcement officials understandably target their efforts toward nabbing the big suppliers, individuals shouldn't think they can't get caught. Their chances of being apprehended are probably low if the anabolic steroids are only for their own use, but that might be changing. Some agencies see arresting anyone in possession of steroids as a way to get information about the other links in the supply chain. In these post-9/11 times, law enforcement officers are taking very close looks at vehicles stopped for routine violations or for such things as

Law enforcement may discover steroid possession during routine traffic stops; tolerance for possession of these chemicals has become much lower than it once was.

Steroids—Pumped Up and Dangerous 93

inspection or seatbelt checks. In some states, such as New York, possession of a hypodermic needle is a misdemeanor and can cause police or state patrols to take another look at what might also be in the vehicle.

The 2006 Congressional Hearings

The 2006 congressional hearings on baseball and anabolic steroids were not intended to change the law for everyone. These hearings were meant to let the baseball world know that if it couldn't handle the steroid problem, Congress would. Senator John McCain of Arizona, when he was chairman of the Senate Commerce Committee, warned the head of the players' union,

> Your failure to commit to addressing this issue straight on and immediately will motivate this committee to search for legislative remedies. . . . I don't know what they [the remedies] are. But I can tell you, and the players you represent, the status quo is not acceptable. And we will have to act in some way unless the major league players' union acts in the affirmative and rapid fashion.

Donald Fehr, head of the players' union, blamed an inability to act on the collective bargaining agreement currently in force. He did point out that testing for 2006 had improved over the previous year. Now positive results could result in punishments, including suspension.

Baseball isn't the only professional sport facing problems with steroids and other performance-enhancing substances. Football has also had a problem, but members of the Senate committee held that sport up as an example

In Canada, steroids are also a controlled substance with penalties that include fines and imprisonment. One of the biggest problems Canada faces with steroids is the illegal shipments of the substances into the country. In 2003, the Canada Border Services Agency (CBSA) reported that most of the illegal shipments originated in the United States. Between 1999 and 2002, there were 390 seizures of steroid shipments that came into Canada from the United States; 48 percent of all the steroid seizures during that time. Most shipments came through the mail. Most of the seizures involved small quantities intended for personal use rather than for sale.

of what *should* be taking place. In football, the commissioner's office and the players' union are working together to solve the problem. In baseball, however, the current policy came about through compromise, with each side having to make concessions. According to committee members, that makes the policy virtually ineffective.

Ordinarily, Congress would not have the authority to force a business to do something about a problem such as steroid abuse. However, because teams travel between states and even between countries, Major League Baseball must comply with the conditions of federal anti-trust laws, which makes it fall under the jurisdiction of Congress.

U.S. Department of Justice, Drug Enforcement Administration Drug Schedule

Schedule I

- The drug or other substance has a high potential for abuse.
- The drug or other substance has no currently accepted medical use in treatment in the United States.
- There is a lack of accepted safety for use of the drug or other substance under medical supervision.
- Some Schedule I substances are heroin, LSD, marijuana, and methaqualone.

Schedule II

- The drug or other substance has a high potential for abuse.
- The drug or other substance has a currently accepted medical use in treatment in the United States or a currently accepted medical use with severe restrictions.
- Abuse of the drug or other substance may lead to severe psychological or physical dependence.
- Schedule II substances include morphine, PCP, cocaine, methadone, and methamphetamine.

Schedule III

- The drug or other substance has a potential for abuse less than the drugs or other substances in Schedules I and II.
- The drug or other substance has a currently accepted medical use in treatment in the United States.
- Abuse of the drug or other substance may lead to moderate or low physical dependence or high psychological dependence.
- Anabolic steroids, codeine and hydrocodone with aspirin or Tylenol, and some barbiturates are Schedule III substances.

Schedule IV

- The drug or other substance has a low potential for abuse relative to the drugs or other substances in Schedule III.
- The drug or other substance has a currently accepted medical use in treatment in the United States.
- Abuse of the drug or other substance may lead to limited physical dependence or psychological dependence relative to the drugs or other substances in Schedule III.
- Included in Schedule IV are Darvon, Talwin, Equanil, Valium and Xanax.

Schedule V

- The drug or other substance has a low potential for abuse relative to the drugs or other substances in Schedule IV.
- The drug or other substance has a currently accepted medical use in treatment in the United States.
- Abuse of the drug or other substance may lead to limited physical dependence or psychological dependence relative to the drugs or other substances in Schedule IV.
- Over-the-counter cough medicines with codeine are classified in Schedule V.

6 Different Paths— Similar Results: Alternatives to Steroids

Steroids and other performance-enhancing substances are not good for your health. You could get thrown into jail for using them. Even the U.S. Congress is against them. But you want to perform at your optimum level—be the best you can be—and it doesn't seem as though hard work and practice are going to be enough. There have to be some alternatives, right?

Of course there are alternatives. And you shouldn't be too quick to rule out the tried and true. The American Association of Pediatrics (www.aap.org) recommends the following:

- Train safely, without using drugs.
- Eat a healthy diet.
- Get plenty of rest.

Working out with a trained professional can help you achieve the goals you're looking for.

100 Chapter 6—Different Paths—Similar Results

- Set realistic goals and be proud of yourself when you reach them.
- Seek out training supervision, coaching, and advice from a reliable professional.
- Avoid injuries by playing safely and using protective gear.
- Talk to your pediatrician about nutrition, your health, preventing injury, and safe ways to gain strength.

If those aren't enough, there are other substances available. However, many of them have their negative sides as well.

Setting yourself realistic goals is an important part of any healthy fitness program.

Creatine

One of the most popular products among young athletes, their coaches, trainers, and even parents is creatine. Advertisements boast of its "naturalness" and its ability to make the user bigger and stronger, two key words in the minds of adolescent athletes.

Creatine is a nutrient, an essential amino acid, the product of other amino acids. Outside the body, it is found in such foods as fish, milk, and meat.

Studies of adults taking creatine do show some increased muscle size. However, it appears to be caused by fluid retention. It has also been seen to increase power for short-term sports, such as sprinting, though there is no evidence that it is beneficial for endurance sports.

Meat and fish are two good natural sources of creatine, an amino acid.

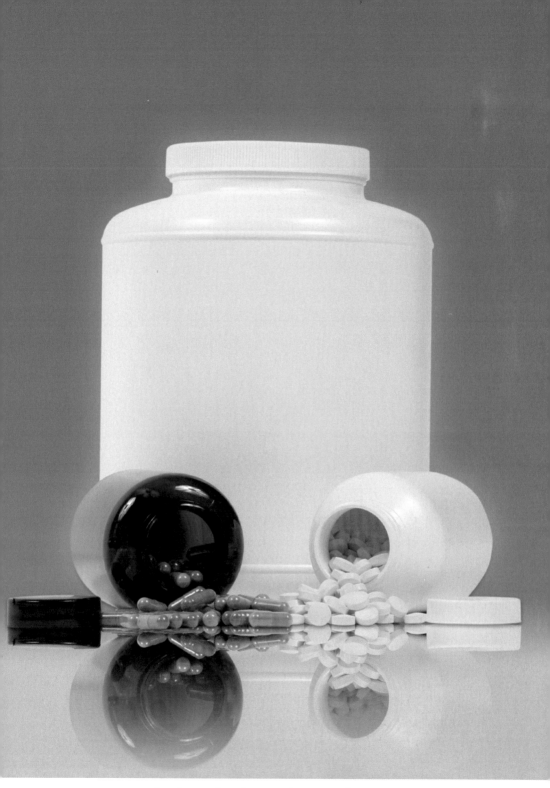

Creatine can be taken as a dietary supplement.

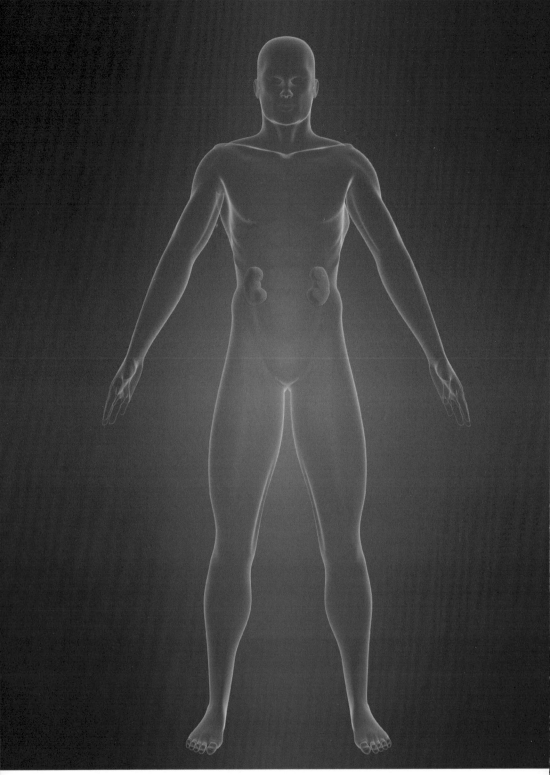

Because creatine can cause dehydration, it can put stress on kidneys that may be dangerous.

Although it might be a "natural product," creatine does have its downside. First, its use as a performance-enhancing drug has not received much scientific study. Because of that, it is not possible to know what long-term effects it might have. Optimum dosages—and more important, the excessive dosage—have not been determined. Because the FDA does not regulate creatine products, it is impossible to vouch for their purity; no one would know for sure what she was putting into her body.

Side effects of taking creatine include

- abdominal pain
- nausea
- loose stools
- weight gain due to water retention
- muscle cramps
- muscle strains

Anecdotal evidence indicates that dehydration can occur when creatine is taken while athletes exercise in very hot weather. Kidney function and heart enlargement have been seen among children who take creatine. Taking supplemental creatine causes the body to make less of its own creatine, but researchers do not know what (if any) long-term effects this might cause.

DHEA

Nutritional centers and even gyms have promoted the use of dehydroepiandrosterone, more commonly known as DHEA. DHEA is a chemical related to the sex hormones testosterone and estrogen and is found in the *adrenal glands*.

The ads for this substance might remind you of the patent medicines discussed in chapter 1. DHEA has been claimed to increase muscle mass and strength, ease depression, prevent heart disease, and increase libido. No wonder it's a popular supplement, especially for older athletes looking for the edge that age might have worn off.

Individuals taking DHEA have found themselves facing many of the side effects shared with anabolic steroids. Women have reported increased hair growth, and the incidence of endometrial cancer is increased in women who have taken DHEA. Men who have taken DHEA

Follow safety guidelines if you choose to embark on a weight-training program.

Eight Basic Rules for Strength Training

1. Start with body weight exercises for a few weeks (such as sit-ups, push-ups, and pull-ups) before using weights.
2. Work out with weights about three times a week. Avoid weight training on back-to-back days.
3. Warm up for 5–10 minutes before each session.
4. Stretch the muscles you plan to strengthen before each weight training session.
5. Spend no more than 40 minutes in the weight room to avoid fatigue or boredom.
6. Work more reps; avoid maximum lifts.
7. Ensure you're using proper technique through supervision. Improper technique may result in injuries, particularly in the shoulder and back.
8. Cool down for 5–10 minutes after each session, stretching the muscles you worked out.

(*Source*: TeensHealth, www.kidshealth.org)

may find themselves with permanently enlarged breasts and an increased chance of developing prostate cancer. Most experts recommend that everyone—adults and children—not use DHEA.

Ephedra

Ephedra- and ephedrine-containing dietary supplements have proven to be among the most dangerous of all. These products include ma huang, Chinese ephedra, and Sida cordifolia. Ephedrine-containing products and Xenedrine are advertised to improve athletic performance and to dramatically increase weight loss.

Structurally, there's not much difference between ephedrine and amphetamines. Ephedrine stimulates the central nervous system (the brain and spinal cord) and works as a decongestant. Though it is an effective treatment for bronchial asthma, it can cause a dangerous *tachycardia* and increases blood pressure. The FDA and state medical boards have received information on more than eight hundred "injuries" due to ephedrine-containing products. More than fifty deaths have been linked to the supplement, most caused by heart attacks, strokes, or *intracranial bleeding*.

Unlike DHEA, the FDA has control over ephedra. In 2004, the FDA banned sales of products that contained ephedra. It is now illegal to buy or sell supplements that contain ephedra, including ephedrine.

Ephedrine's side effects include:

- heart attack
- stroke
- seizures
- psychosis
- death
- dizziness
- headache
- gastrointestinal distress
- irregular heartbeat, including tachycardia
- heart palpitations

Nondrug Alternatives

Taking steroids or performance-enhancing supplements is not the only way to increase muscle mass and athletic ability.

Strength Training

An effective exercise program includes aerobic exercise to make your muscles use oxygen more efficiently (thereby

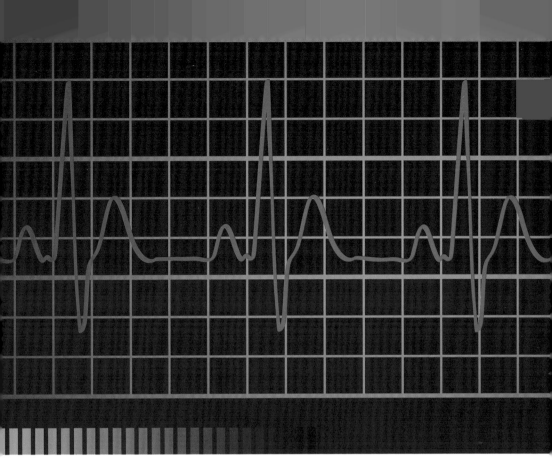
Ephedra can cause abnormal heart rhythms.

making your heart and lungs stronger) and strength training, which increases strength and muscle mass. Strength training is particularly good for women, as it helps prevent *osteoporosis*.

When you participate in a strength-training program, you use weights to add resistance; your muscles are required to work harder because of the extra weight. Two types of weights are used. Free weights, such as hand weights, ankle weights, and barbells, work the members of a group of muscles at one time. To work on a single muscle, weight machines are generally used. If you're using weights machines at a gym, they'll most likely be set up in a specific pattern of exercises that allow you

Exercising with weights can be an effective way to build muscles.

Chapter 6—Different Paths—Similar Results

to work on different muscles. If you don't have access to weights, resistance bands can be used in strength training. You can also use your own body as resistance—try pushups or push yourself away from a surface, such as a wall.

Before beginning strength training, or any program involving weights, be certain to have a thorough checkup. Find an experienced coach or trainer to show you how to warm up and cool down properly, as well as the correct way to use free weights and the weight machines. Remember, the idea is to have a fluid motion when moving the weights, not try to see how quickly you can jerk the weight up. That's a good way to get hurt—not fit.

Food

Eating well is another way to be all you can be. Active people generally need more calories than their **sedentary** peers. This means that the athlete can eat more, somewhere between 2,000 and 5,000 calories a day.

Adolescence is a period of growth, and limiting food intake can harm development and lead to lifelong problems. Unless a teen is seriously overweight, he should not diet. This is true for teen athletes as well. Participants in gymnastics, wrestling, and other such sports may be pressured to lose weight—to weigh less than they should. Every request that you "lose a few pounds to be more competitive" should be discussed openly with parents and a physician or nutritionist knowledgeable in the dietary needs of adolescents.

A daily caloric intake of 2,000 to 5,000 for the adolescent athlete is not a green light to eat whatever he wants.

To be beneficial to athletic performance, these calories must come from the right kinds of foods. Some rules to follow in food selection are:

1. Don't eat just one kind of food. Forget about loading up on carbohydrates to prepare for a big game. Your body needs a variety of foods as each has its own benefits.

2. Remember your vitamins and minerals. Many people believe they need to take a vitamin and mineral supplement to receive all they need for the day—but if a person eats a balanced diet, in most cases the supplements aren't necessary. Eating a variety of fruits and vegetables ("Strive for 5") each day helps make sure the body receives the vitamins it needs to function well. Calcium, found in dairy products (low-fat, preferably) and dark green, leafy vegetables, builds and strengthens bones. Lean red meat, leafy greens, and some grains provide iron necessary to build muscle and keep it oxygenated.

3. Eat your protein—but not too much. Protein is necessary to building and maintaining strong, healthy muscles, and teen athletes do need more protein than the average teenager. But both the athlete and the nonathlete alike probably get all the protein they need through foods such as lean meats, poultry, eggs, low-fat dairy products, **legumes**, soy, and peanut butter. Protein powders and protein shakes are not necessary in most cases. Too much protein can cause serious health problems, including dehydration and kidney disorders. Vegetarians must be care-

A healthy diet includes foods from all the major groups: proteins, carbohydrates, fruits and vegetables, fats and oils.

ful to make certain they are eating enough protein since they do not eat meat, and some don't consume eggs, fish, or dairy products either. Beans, legumes, soy, and peanut butter can help vegetarians meet their protein requirements.

4. Don't fall into the no carb, low carb trap. People need to eat foods from all of the food groups, including carbohydrates. The body needs carbohydrates for fuel. The not-so-difficult trick is to eat the right kind of carbs. Complex carbs are good and give you energy over the long haul. Simple carbs are not so good. You'll get a quick rush of energy, but it depletes just as quickly. Simple carbs include sugary foods. They

Beans are a good source of protein for vegetarians.

Warning

Supplements such as creatine and androstenedione ("andro") are gaining popularity. Though these supplements are not steroids, manufacturers claim they can build muscles, and improve strength and stamina, without the side effects of steroids.

It is important to know that these substances are not safe. The FDA has banned the sale of all supplements that contain androstenedione. The FDA has not, however, regulated products containing creatine. Like steroids, both substances are also banned by the NFL, NCAA, and International Olympic Committee.

Although both creatine and androstenedione occur naturally in foods, there are serious concerns about the long-term effects of using them as supplements. These products may be unsafe. Remember, there is no replacement for a healthy diet, proper training, and practice.

taste good, but there have little nutritional value; some people call them empty calories. Complex carbohydrates include whole grains, brown rice, sweet potatoes, corn, and peas. These foods are generally not processed as much as white foods—white bread, white rice. The energy and fiber found in complex carbohydrates can help the athlete have the energy to perform her best.

5. Fatty foods are not necessarily bad. But not all fat is created equal. Individuals should eat limited amounts of fat in general. Unsaturated fat found in vegetable oil is healthier than saturated fat, which comes from animal products. How can you quickly tell the difference? Saturated fat is solid at room temperature.

Fats provide muscles with a long-lasting source of food. However, athletes must be careful about *when* they eat products containing fat. Fat slows down digestion and can make you feel sluggish. So avoid fatty foods for a few hours before competing or even practicing or exercising.

6. Water, water everywhere. Drink it. It is easy for an athlete to become dehydrated. A dehydrated athlete is an ineffective athlete.

Some experts say that individuals should drink six to eight glasses of water a day. That may be right for some, but not all. How much water one should drink depends on age, size, activity level, and **ambient** temperature.

Experts agree that athletes should drink before, during, and after exercise. However, there have been news reports about athletes becoming ill, even dying, from drinking too much water. So monitor your water intake. Drink only what you need; don't force yourself to drink in excess.

As for sports drinks, unless you're exercising for more than ninety minutes in very hot weather, they are of no more benefit than plain water. If you're more likely to actually drink them than you are the water, then you should. The most important thing is to stay hydrated.

Caffeinated drinks should be avoided when exercising or competing, especially in hot weather. They can actually speed up dehydration. Carbonated beverages and juices may cause stomach discomfort if consumed while competing.

It is human nature to want to be the best. And the desire to take shortcuts is also human nature. Unfortunately, when it comes to gaining muscles and strength, or losing weight and appearing more toned, shortcuts can be

Drinking plenty of water is a sensible part of any exercise program.

A Quiz

True or False

1. Many people smoke or inhale steroids.
2. Anabolic steroids can affect the hypothalamus and the limbic region of the brain.
3. Anabolic steroids strengthen the immune system.
4. Anabolic steroids can cause males' breasts to grow and females' breasts to shrink.

Answers:
1. False; 2. True; 3. False; 4. True

(*Source:* NIDA for Teens. http://teens.drugabuse.gov/mom/mom_ster5.asp)

deadly. The best way, and safest, is to do it right—practice, exercise, and eat right. This approach might not bring fast results—but when the results come, you'll be healthy enough to enjoy them.

Glossary

abstinence: The act of completely doing without something, such as a drug.

adrenal glands: Endocrine glands located above each kidney that secrete steroids.

ambient: Existing or present on all sides.

anecdotal evidence: Evidence based on secondhand reports rather than firsthand knowledge, experience, or scientific investigation.

cholesterol: A steroid alcohol found in animal tissue, bile, blood, eggs, and fat.

clitoral hypertrophy: An unusual and excessive enlargement of the clitoris in females.

commiserate: To express sympathy or sorrow.

concurrent: Occurring at the same time.

delusions: False beliefs held despite contrary evidence.

derivatives: Things that have developed from other, similar things.

efficacy: The ability to do what is desired.

gender dysmorphia: A condition in which an individual feels trapped in the body of the wrong gender.

hypogonadism: A condition in which a reproductive gland is smaller than what is considered normal.

hypoplastic anemias: A deficiency of all of the blood's elements, caused by the bone marrow's inability to make enough cells; also called aplastic anemia.

impotence: The inability of a male to achieve or maintain a penile erection.

intracranial bleeding: Bleeding that occurs within the skull.

intramuscularly: Injected into the muscle.

legumes: Seeds, pods, or roots that are used as food.

libido: Sex drive.

lipids: Any of a group of organic compounds consisting of fats, oils, and related substances.

mania: A psychiatric disorder characterized by excessive physical activity, rapidly changing ideas, and impulsive behavior.

osteoporosis: A disease of postmenopausal women in which bones lose their density, becoming brittle.

pharmacological: Relating to the science or study of drugs.

placebo: A substance with no active ingredients.

relapses: Instances in which an individual returns to previous behaviors.

sedentary: Involving a lot of sitting and little exercise.

serendipitously: A favorable occurrence that happens by accident.

solvent: A substance in which other substances can be dissolved.

sublingual: Administered by placing under the tongue.

synthetic: Not natural.

tachycardia: Excessively rapid heartbeat.

transcend: Go beyond.

transdermal: Administered through the skin, such as by a patch.

Western: Typical of countries, especially in Europe and North and South America, whose culture and society are influenced by Greek and Roman culture and Christianity.

Further Reading

American Medical Association. *Boy's Guide to Becoming a Teen.* San Francisco: Jossey-Bass, 2006.

Aretha, David. *Steroids and Other Performance-Enhancing Drugs.* Berkeley Heights, N.J.: Enslow, 2005.

Bailes, Julian, and John McClosky. *When Winning Costs Too Much: Steroids, Supplements, and Scandal in Today's Sports World.* New York: Taylor Trade, 2005.

Connolly, Sean. *Steroids.* Portsmouth, N.H.: Heinemann, 2000.

Egendorf, Laura K. *Steroids.* Farmington Hills, Mich.: Greenhaven, 2005.

Esherick, Joan. *Dying for Acceptance: A Teen's Guide to Drug- and Alcohol-Related Health Issues.* Broomall, Pa.: Mason Crest, 2005.

Fainaru-Wada, Mark, and Lance Williams. *Game of Shadows: Barry Bonds, BALCO, and the Steroids Scandal that Rocked Professional Sports.* New York: Penguin, 2006.

Fitzhugh, Karla. *Steroids (What's the Deal?).* Portsmouth, N.H.: Heinemann, 2005.

Hovius, Christopher. *The Best You Can Be: A Teen's Guide to Fitness and Nutrition.* Broomall, Pa.: Mason Crest, 2005.

Jendrick, Nathan. *Dunks, Doubles, Doping: How Steroids Are Killing American Athletics.* New York: Lyons Press, 2006.

Levert, Suzanne. *The Facts About Steroids.* New York: Benchmark, 2004.

Lukas, Scott E. *Steroids.* Berkeley Heights, N.J.: Enslow, 2001.

Mintzer, Richard. *Steroids = Busted!* Berkeley Heights, N.J.: Enslow, 2006.

Monroe, Judy. *Steroids, Sports, and Body Image: The Risks of Performance-Enhancing Drugs.* Berkeley Heights, N.J.: Enslow, 2004.

Rutstein, Jeff. *The Steroid Deceit: A Body Worth Dying For?* New York: Custom Fitness, 2006.

Santella, Thomas M. *Body Enhancement Products.* New York: Chelsea House, 2005.

Simons, Rae. *For All to See: A Teen's Guide to Healthy Skin.* Broomall, Pa.: Mason Crest, 2005.

Spring, Albert. *Steroids and Your Muscles: The Incredibly Disgusting Story.* New York: Rosen, 2001.

Yesalis, Charles E., and Virginia S. Cowart. *The Steroids Game.* New York: Human Kinetics, 2000.

For More Information

Play Safe, Play Fair
www.aap.org/family/steroids.htm

Teenbodybuilding.com
www.teenbodybuilding.com/derek4.htm

Tips for Teens: Steroids
www.ncadi.samhsa.gov/govpubs/PHD726

The websites listed on this page were active at the time of publication. The publisher is not responsible for websites that have changed their addresses or discontinued operation since the date of publication. The publisher will review and update the website list upon each reprint.

Bibliography

Collins, Rick. "Anabolic Steroids and the Athlete: The Legal Issues." http://www.mesomorphosis.com/articles/colins/anabolic-steroids-and-the-law.htm.

Dowshen, Steven. "Are Steroids Worth the Risk?" http://www.kidshealth.org/teen/drug_alcohol/drugs/steroids.html.

Greydanus, Donald E. "Sports Doping: What Should Parents Know?" http://www.coolnurse.healthology.com/focus_article.asp?f=teenhealth&c=teen_doping.

Missouri Department of Mental Health, Division of Alcohol and Drug Abuse. "As a Matter of Fact . . . Steroids." http://www.well.com/user/woa/fsroids.htm.

National Institute on Drug Abuse. "Consequences of the Abuse of Anabolic Steroids." http://drugabuse.gov/about/welcome/message-steroids305.html.

National Institute on Drug Abuse. *NIDA InfoFacts: Steroids (Anabolic-Androgenic)*. Washington, D.C.: U.S. Department of Health and Human Services, National Institutes of Health, 2005.

National Institute on Drug Abuse. *NIDA InfoFacts: High School and Youth Trends*. Washington, D.C.: U.S. Department of Health and Human Services, National Institutes of Health, 2006.

National Institute on Drug Abuse. *Research Report: Anabolic Steroid Abuse*. Washington, D.C.: U.S. Department of Health and Human Services, National Institutes of Health, 2006.

NIDA for Teens. "Mind Over Matter: Anabolic Steroids." http://teens.drugabuse.gov/mom/mom_ster4.asp.

Puma, Mike. "Not the Size of the Dog in the Fight." *ESPN Classic*. http://www.go.com/classic/biography/s/Alzado_Lyle.html.

"Steroids: Play Safe, Play Fair." http://www.aap.org/family/steroids.htm.

"Teens and Anabolic Steroids." http://www.focusas.com/Steroids.html.

"Teens and Steroids." http://www.teendrugabuse.us/teensteroids.html.

"Teens & Steroids: A Dangerous Mix." *CBS News*, June 3, 2004.

TeensHealth. "A Guide to Eating for Sports." http://www.kidshealth.org/teen/food_fitness/nutrition/eatnrun.html.

Tohidi, Ramin. "Anabolic Steroids: A Look at Potential Drug Testing Legislation and Its Constitutional Implications." http://www.leda.law.harvard.edu/leda/data/791/Tohidi06.html.

Zaccardi, Nick. "Anabolic Steroids." *WellnessMD*. http://www.wellnessmd.com/anabolics.html.

Index

Picture Credits

Author and Consultant Biographies

Author

Ida Walker is a graduate of the University of Northern Iowa in Cedar Falls, and has done graduate work at Syracuse University in Syracuse, New York. The author of several nonfiction books, she lives in Upstate New York.

Series Consultant

Jack E. Henningfield, Ph.D., is a professor at the Johns Hopkins University School of Medicine, and he is also Vice President for Research and Health Policy at Pinney Associates, a consulting firm in Bethesda, Maryland, that specializes in science policy and regulatory issues concerning public health, medications development, and behavior-focused disease management. Dr. Henningfield has contributed information relating to addiction to numerous reports of the U.S. Surgeon General, the National Academy of Sciences, and the World Health Organization.